When Gertrude Came, I Wasn't Home

Musings on My Early Life

Vincent L. Marando

When Gertrude Came, I Wasn't Home

© 2021 Vincent I. Marando

Paperback ISBN: 978-1-66780-100-1
eBook ISBN: 978-1-66780-101-8

To former, current and future family generations.

To the memory of Joseph and Grace Marando, my parents.

Patti my wife. I would not be the person I have become without her love, support and tolerance.

Marianne, Shelley, Melissa, daughters who have made life a joy.

Kirsten, VJ (Vincent Joseph) Anthony, grandchildren who are truly wonderful adults.

Bella Snraia, A great granddaughter who has a world to explore.

CONTENTS

ACKNOWLEDGEMENTS

Mary Beth Melchior assisted me much more than writing the Foreword to my Memoir. As an editor she made my stiff sentences a flowing narrative. Mary Beth researched and wrote the section about Gertrude that is in the Appendix. Without her assistance my memoir would not have had the quality and substance it now possesses.

Barbara Morrison offered valuable guidance and comments on the overall approach I took in my memoir. Herta Feely and Emily Williamson read sections of memoir and provided valuable comments. James Corsaro read the entire manuscript and offered insightful comments throughout, especially on the immigrant Italian culture in Western New York. Paul Hirsch provided addition insights about the era of world war II and city life after the War. Frances Schmidt offered insightful observation about Buffalo's West Side the process of publishing. Scribner Messenger read an overview critique of my book as well as specific editorial comments. Sayna Blank provide a critical overview of the book.

Keith Harries provided keen observations on the entire manuscript and especially about the similarity of games played in England and the US in the 1940s and 50s.

Samuele F.S. Pardini offered insight into assessing Italian ethnicity In America; and described the destruction of Buffalo's system of parks by highway construction.

Mark and Shelley Stout proofread the entire manuscript.

The following offered comments on content and corrected sentence and editorial errors: Charles Sternheim, Leo Kennedy. Marianne Hanson and Melissa Henningsen.

Joe Di Leo, Publisher of *Per Niente Magazine* offed guidance and support throughout the project

Cynthia Van Ness of the Buffalo and Erie County Society provided Historical verification of facts and Photos of Buffalo.

Of course, I am responsible for any errors and misrepresentations.

FOREWORD

You may not know Vincent "Vince" Marando, but you would be glad if you did. Vince looks a bit like Tony Bennett, he's lots of fun, and he's a heck of a good cook. He's a great guy to spend an evening with – you'll eat good food, drink good wine, and have interesting conversation.

But that's not why you should read this book.

This book will let you begin to know Vince Marando – and in getting to know Vince Marando, you'll get to know America a little better, too. And you will get some insight into how much – and how little – the U.S. has changed over the course of the last 80 years.

In this volume, you will read about what Vince calls the "long decade" of the 1940s – from 1938 to 1952. The catalyst for Vince's ruminations on his past and our crazy present was the release of the data from the U.S. Census of 1940. This is the first touchpoint connecting then and now – the Census was conducted in 2020, just as it was in 1940.

Of course, Vince was not even two years old when Gertrude K. Bunce, the 1940 Census enumerator, came to his home. So how does he remember this?

Vince was just 18 months old on April 4, 1940 when Gertrude Bunce, Census Enumerator, arrived at his family's home. When the 1940 Census was released to the public in 2012 – listing the names of his family and neighbors – it allowed him to "almost" enter his world the way it was at that time. Vince started doing research on his family, his community, and the lives of those who raised him.

So, Vince began to write. And after he had been writing for a while, it became clearer that he was not just writing about his life, his past – he was writing about the intersection of *our* past, and *our* present. As the research progressed, he realized something: that little boy's life spoke to so much of what is going on in our 21st century American lives. While on the surface it seemed like everything had changed, there was plenty that hadn't changed, and much from that time that was coming to the forefront again.

It was quite fascinating: Vince's life was interesting enough on its own, but as he wrote, more and more parallels between the 1940s and the 21st century became evident. Exploring the ways that the past and the present were shedding light on each other became not only easy, but virtually unavoidable.

Take, for instance, immigration: Vince's maternal grandparents and his father were all immigrants from southern Italy (specifically, Sicily and Calabria). In the 1940s, Italians were considered among the lower class of immigrants to the U.S. – and on top of that, Vince's father came to the country illegally. Indeed, when Vince was a teenager the family spent three summers picking green beans and berries on a farm outside of Buffalo with other Italian immigrant families – work that is primarily done now by Hispanic immigrant laborers, who have taken up that lower rung on the immigration ladder as Italian immigrants have climbed higher.

Vince's exploration of what it meant to be raised in an immigrant household in Buffalo in the 1940s suggests that not much has changed in the intervening years – immigrant families still tend to live in multi-generational households where the children speak more English than the adults in the family. Italian then, Spanish now... but English outside the home and native language at home continues to be the pattern. In addition, living conditions for many immigrant families still remain cramped;

and immigrants generally have limited job opportunities that are largely defined by their network.

The parallels between the Italian immigrants of that era and the Hispanic immigrants of the present seem to offer a glimmer of hope that America will work through the toxicity that surrounds so much of the discussion of immigration today. But of course this won't "just happen" – and it is hard to see how building a wall between us and our neighbors to the south will speed this process along. What is notable, though, is that the complex relationship between the "tired... poor... huddled masses yearning to breathe free" and Americans whose families came to these shores some time before the latest arrivals was not substantially easier in the time of Vince's childhood than it is now.

What has most definitely changed is today's access to information and our relationship to media: Vince didn't have his own radio, and his family didn't have access to a television until he was a young teen. His "screen time" consisted of going to the movies once a week. The newsreels of the era told him of Allied victories in the Second World War, which he and his friends turned into games children played – one team being the "America good guys," the other being the "Nazi bad guys." There was "us" and "them" – but the villains were not living in our country.

The depth of the difference between the ways that information was transmitted in the 1940s and the way this works now is highlighted in the constant bombardment of "Breaking News." In the 1940s radio, movies and TV, with three networks, provided the news at 6 and 11PM – if you even had a televison. There were no 24 hour a day channels to remind young Vince that the government thought his father was a "problem" – or that suggested to him that he was less of an American because one of his parents had not been born in the United States.

And then there's the question of privacy, which has also changed over the decades. Having no privacy in 1940 meant sharing a bedroom and one bathroom. Today, the lack of privacy is largely a digital phenomenon.

Nothing is easily erased; photos and conversations remain available long after those who were involved have forgotten about their existence. This change in the understanding of what constitutes "privacy" – and other words whose meanings have changed across the decades – plays a central role in this book. The "generation gap" in communication has been a challenge for much of the last 100 years, and it isn't going away.

But to only focus on the gap itself is to miss what has fallen into that gap – for example, today's young people worry about their photos being misused, but do they even know that they are missing out on the kind of privacy that lets them make mistakes and learn how to fix them without parental intrusion? Does the lack of physical privacy in childhood make it more difficult for the younger generations to develop the discernment that lets them know when to ask for help, and when to tough it out alone? And how can that knowledge be gained if there is no recognition that it may have been lost?

Making those decisions and learning those skills was just a part of being a kid when Vince was a child, and he gives us many funny, compelling stories that highlight both the joy and the potential hazards of gaining this wisdom. Was it all worth it? That is for the reader to decide.

When we take the time to read about a time gone by, it is easy to romanticize it: things were "simpler," people had more "common sense," and the world was just better. Of course, that is just the view from our perspective now – it did not seem that way to the people living in that moment. Vince takes the time to explore this phenomenon in various big and small ways throughout this volume. From reflecting on the different parts of Buffalo he became exposed to as he was growing up, to considering how federally-subsidized housing in his childhood neighborhood did not have the stigma it has now, Vince highlights how "common sense" isn't really all that *common* – it's just a function of growing up in a particular family, in a particular place, at a particular time. And he suggests that the idea of common sense is going to seem to fall apart for most everyone at a certain point.

This is an important insight – because it takes the idea that there was something that was fixed and shared and *real* and that is now gone, and says we need to reconsider that. Common sense is not something that *we had* and that is now lost, taken away from us somehow by someone or something.

Indeed, Vince seems to suggest that common sense is a function of being a child – and it is time for us to grow up. And by that I don't just mean we need to grow up as individuals; in reading the stories Vince lays out here, I would argue that it becomes clear that it is time for us to grow up *as a nation* – to stop whining because our world is no longer the simple world of a child. It's time for America – all of us – to stand tall and figure out what it's going to take to live effectively in the current reality. Yes, the world is chaotic. People see things differently and in ways that will often make no sense from our own perspectives. But it is our job as *adults* (and as an adult nation) to take this in not with anger, but with the understanding that our "common sense" looks just as crazy to someone else as theirs does to us.

But Vince also makes an interesting and quite subtle point in discussing this: the "common sense" given to children in families is a foundation, and if that foundation is smashed too soon or too fast, that can create its own problems. In these musings, we see how the "common sense" of the Marando/Gardo families starts to come apart in pieces and over time: Vince sees a friend take money out of the church offering envelope to buy potato chips for himself; he sees another friend throw out the meat in a sandwich; he meets swimmers who are planning for college – something no one in his neighborhood discusses. His worldview changes – but it changes slowly over time.

Vince contrasts this with the pressure to expand their worldview that today's young people are under, as scores of images from social media flood their consciousness long before they are able to integrate that information effectively into the world that physically surrounds them. While he makes no suggestions about the impact of this on a young mind, it serves as a reminder to the reader that it is important to carefully and thoughtfully build a foundation – and to give that foundation time to settle before trying to put the weight of the world on it. There is a vast difference between sheltering our children and working with a young mind in a way that is appropriate and supportive of growth and development.

And that leads us to another important twist to this story, one that ties together the ideas of common sense and privacy in a striking – and totally unexpected – way. Vince begins this book with the visit of the 1940 census taker, Gertrude K. Bunce – but as the title says, when Gertrude came to his house, Vince was not there. Vince was actually in the hospital at that time, dealing with that era's pandemic – polio. And as he was finishing the writing of this volume, America began its journey with another pandemic – COVID-19.

And this parallel may be where the reader can most clearly see how America is still the same, and how it has become a very different nation over the course of Vince's lifetime. The similarity is clear: as a nation and as individuals, we are still susceptible to disease and death, and we cannot fix the problems that adhere to illness with a stroke of a pen or by just willing them away. In 1939, almost 8,000 children in the United States contracted polio, and just over 800 of them died. Vince Marando was one of those children who got the disease – and lucky for us, he was one of the ones who made it.

Polio was an epidemic at that time, and as you'll read, it caused people to fear each other, and the attempt to prevent its spread caused the closure of schools, swimming pools and many other enterprises that catered to the gathering of children and families during those years. Life was not the same as it had been before the polio epidemic started. Yet – eventually – polio became a disease relegated to the past.

But illness is illness, and as with polio, so with Covid-19: everyone is willing to do whatever it takes to bring this pandemic under control, right? Well, not exactly. And this is where Vince shows us how American society has really changed.

Covid-19 has absolutely illuminated a massive change in American life over the course of the last 80 years: we no longer have shared truths, and many Americans don't truly trust our institutions and experts or have faith in our democratic system of governing. During the 1940s there was national unity because the U.S. was facing external threats; in the 21st century, challenges from the outside have been replaced by the threat of misinformation that foments domestic division.

In the 1940s and 1950s, there was no one demanding that pools be opened in the summer, polio risk be damned. There was no one taking to the streets to demand their liberty to hold a birthday party. There wasn't even anyone proposing that all the iron lungs be thrown away, because it was all a hoax.

There was just a nation of people trying to keep their children safe.

And yes, the scale was totally different. But there was something else that was different, too.

I would suggest what has changed in America is TRUST – trust in our government, trust in our public institutions, trust in our neighbors, and most importantly, trust in our selves. And just as Vince discusses the erosion of common sense over time, so too he allows us to begin to consider the importance of the erosion of trust over time.

Vince wrote so much of this volume with his grandchildren – three fine young adults – in mind, but the erosion of trust is really relevant to all of us. How will we move forward in a world where so many of us don't know the truth from fiction, where we have little trust in our government, our neighbors, and even ourselves?

I would suggest that this volume provides us with some great role modeling: look at the world and acknowledge what you see, even if it's different and difficult. Don't be afraid to ask a lot of questions. And find yourself a good uncle, aunt or teacher – they can make all the difference.

Enjoy diving into Vince's childhood – it may remind you of what you need to create today to make your life (indeed, all of our lives) a bit better.

Mary Beth Melchior, Ph.D.

Western Massachusetts

Summer 2021

PROLOGUE: A VISITOR ARRIVES

Gertrude Bunce, U.S. Census Enumerator, entered Buffalo's West Side, an Italian village, on Thursday, April 4, 1940, and came to visit my home. The names she recorded were Italian – indeed, the names she recorded in most of the neighborhood were from a particular region of Italy – Sicily. "The West Side" was a coded reference to "the place where the Sicilians lived" – a designation that everyone who knew it understood as "the people who were near the bottom of the social ladder among Italian immigrants" and the "people who were likely to be Mafioso."

Gertrude was a strange name. No one in my neighborhood, and certainly no one in my family, would have known anyone named Gertrude. The name was foreign – which is to say, it was not Italian. She recorded my family and me.

I have written what I would have liked Gertrude and others to know.

If Gertrude had been more than an enumerator, and instead had had the opportunity to learn about my family and me, she would have become aware of the journey of a working-class Italian immigrant family. She would have noted how I, the son of an immigrant, eventually would have to negotiate and adapt to America, striving to learn and accept a "foreign" culture.

What did Gertrude think of the responses to the questions she asked at my house? I wish I could talk to Gertrude, to get her thoughts on my family and my neighborhood.[1]

Gertrude reported three separate households living at 412 Busti Avenue.[2] I lived in one of those, which was a household connected to two other homes that were always open and welcoming to me. From my perspective, all three households were my family. My nuclear and extended family were one.

And so, my current perspective on the public edition of the 1940 U.S. Census was quite different from how Gertrude reported the data. My family was not living in three discrete "households." We were interlinked and interdependent. I was as likely to be disciplined or rewarded by any of my relatives as I was by my mother and father.

Furthermore, the Census reported my family as being immigrants and first-generation Americans. Of course, when I read the 2012 public edition of the U.S. Census, I recognized the names of all the people she recorded – but I also noted that one of my uncles was not reported. I will never know why Great Uncle Sam was not mentioned – Nonna (my grandmother) and Aunt Rose (the Census respondents) took that information with them to their graves.

Gertrude recorded us as *data*. She was an "outsider," a non-Italian who did not know us. Gertrude might never have visited the Buffalo's West Side without this official purpose. It was Gertrude's signature on the

---

1 Gertrude died in September 1972 – 40 years before I would become aware of her visit to my home. (https://www.ancientfaces.com/person/gertrude-bunce-birth-1890-death-1972/13467986) In the course of researching this book, we were able to find her grandchildren and learn more about her life. See Appendix A.

2 In 1929, what had been Front Street in Buffalo was renamed Busti Avenue after Paulo Busti (1749-1824) who was an Italian immigrant who spoke four languages, including English. He had been in charge of land development for the Holland Land Company's holdings in Western New York. Ironically, Paulo Busti was a northern Italian whereas Busti Avenue consisted mostly of Southern Italians. Busti Avenue in the 1920s had become predominantly a street of Italian residents who moved away from the tenements of Dante Place where they had first located upon arriving in Buffalo in the late 19th and early 20th century.

Census form which stimulated me to reflect on my past – and to begin to write seven decades later, reflecting on how the past and present have seemed to diverge, but aren't really separate.

The family that Gertrude recorded included individuals with distinct personalities and some great "characters" who had profound impacts on my development. The lens of time lets me understand them and the environment they provided me more clearly. And though I now better understand some of their challenges, I know the time has passed where I could begin to comprehend the depth and extent of their feelings as they moved through this new world.

I look back on these documents through the lens of eight decades of experience. As I look at these data, I am struck by the fact that these people had lives and faced challenges which I was too young to grasp. My extended family of more than a dozen persons and I were negotiating life in the 1940s and we looked with positive expectations toward the future. The future I viewed from the 1940's is now the past - and this present moment highlights the ways that everything has changed and how, despite these changes, the challenges of being human still resonate in much the same way.

April 2, 2012

The data from the 1940 Census was released to the National Archives on April 2, 2012 in accordance with the 72-year rule.[3] I have spent my adult life interacting with government documents, and I knew this release of information provided a rare opportunity for me to use my experience as a professor of political science to learn about my personal life – the life that I had lived but that was long past and is, in some ways, inaccessible without this information.

---

3 The original images of these Census pages can be found at: https://www.census.gov/history/www/genealogy/decennial_census_records/the_72_year_rule_1.html

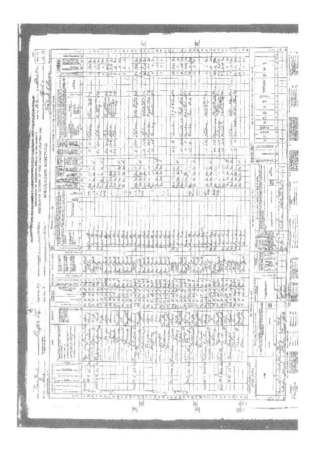

An example of a page from the 1940 recording my family.

This census data stimulated my thinking and desire to probe my past. For me, this was memory supported by selected historical assessments of family members and living conditions in 1940. The data have had a dramatic impact on me, as if I met the persons themselves – again. They were frozen in time, provoking memories and raising questions that I had not yet taken the time to seriously consider.

The 1940's was a pivotal decade for the United States – and for me. Employment in 1940 reflected a needed start to recovery after the decade-long Great Depression. There were growing clouds hinting at a war that would eventually involve the United States. 1940 was the beginning of transition from an economically depressed peacetime to a prosperous economy preparing for a probable war.

The Great Depression had a massive impact on my family, and on most Americans. Most everyone had felt the effects of high unemployment, which had reached 25% during the previous decade. Economic security and the importance of having a job were absolutely critical to my family and to most of the nation's population. When Gertrude came to the door in 1940, the unemployment rate was still at 15% -- the lasting effects of the Depression still lingered. The 1940 census was designed not only to enumerate the population as the U.S. Constitution requires, but also to gather information to better understand the consequences of unemployment and evaluate the progress being made toward improving the economy.

So, I have focused on the 1940s, though I stretch that decade out from my birth year in 1938, to 1952, when I graduated from grammar school. This 14 year "decade" is a period of special meaning to me: it provided the foundation from which I began to recognize moving forward. And I have been astounded to see how many of the dynamics that defined my life – and America – in the 1940s are still resonating today.

I now see a "past" that has evolved into my present – and the present and future that is shaping my grandchildren's lives. The values and social norms to which I – and they – now respond, evolved slowly from my base in the 1940's.

Gertrude, you did your duty and filled out the Census report. You could not have observed me, nor known much more about the persons you reported. The reflections contained in this book provide some description and explanation of those early years – and their continuing resonance in American life here in the 21st century. Thank you, Gertrude, for contributing the stimulus and framework for this project. Thank you for coming to visit my family at 412 Busti Avenue, Buffalo New York. Now, Gertrude, I'd like to provide a little bit more information about the individuals you recorded, and the circumstances in which they lived.

CHAPTER 1:

WHEN GERTRUDE CAME, I WASN'T HOME

When Census Enumerator Gertrude K. Bunce visited 412 Busti Avenue on Buffalo's West Side on Thursday, April 4th, 1940, I suspect she was aware that she had come to an Italian Village. All the names she recorded were Italian – more specifically, Sicilian. Houses had small flower gardens and bushes surrounded by chain-linked fences. There were occasionally trees in front of some homes.[4] Front lawns were quite small – no more than 120 square feet . A mechanical push mower was quite adequate for mowing the grass. All the homes on the block were neatly kept, which was typical of these working-class Italian streets.

The streets and avenues in my neighborhood were laid out on a north-south, east-west grid system. Each block on a street consisted of 15 to 20 houses. Most of the houses on my block were narrow, two-story wood frame houses. Several of the homes had a cottage in the rear: ours did, and this is where my family and I lived. The cottage was referred to as "the house in the back." Only one or two homes had a garage. Autos were parked on the street. There were few families that owned an automobile. My grandfather owned a car and my uncle owned a dump truck that he kept at a separate parking lot.

4 I remember the single tree in front of our home quite well. I dug a hole at its base thinking that if I dug deep enough I would reach China, as I had learned in school that it was on the other side of the world. No one had mentioned how long I would have to dig to get there.

Busti Avenue (probably 1950s). Photo: Buffalo Historical Society.

Busti Avenue was a one-way street, which was considered safer than a two-way street. I was instructed as a youngster to look both ways before crossing the street, even though cars would only be coming from one direction. All I really had to do was look in the direction from which traffic flowed, though as I learned in kindergarten and was reinforced by my family, I was to look both ways.

Located three blocks to the north was the Peace Bridge, which connected the United States to Canada. The terminus of the Peace Bridge was in the magnificent Front Park which bordered the waterfront. Front Park was part of a system of linked parks in Buffalo.[5] What I remember most about the park was the area where Buffalo's Mounted Police unit kept their

---

5 Front Park was part of the "city within a park" design of Frederick Law Olmsted. In 1868, Olmsted was invited to Buffalo in the aftermath of designing Central Park and Prospect Park in New York City. "Inspired by Buffalo's radial street design and also its proximity to Lake Erie and local creeks and waterways, he proposed creating a "city within a park"; his design ended up encompassing six major parks, seven parkways, and eight landscaped circles throughout the city. The country's first urban parks system was born." (https://www. bfloparks.org/buffalos-frederick-law-olmsted-legacy-the-park-system-that-started-it-all/) Delaware Park – part of this system – was near the home we would move to in the mid-1940s, on Grant Street. I would later move to Michigan, where I would encounter another Olmsted park, Detroit's Belle Isle (though Olmsted's relationship with that park was much more contentious than it had been with the City of Buffalo's parks system).

horses in a stable. I and several of my buddies would see many horses, all of which had names, at the stable.[6]

Some of the homes on Busti Avenue near Front Park and Peace Bridge had a view of the waterfront. These homes were larger and more expensive than the homes on my block. Social class among the Italians of Busti Avenue could be gauged by how close they were to Front Park. Mostly, though, the Italian ethnicity shielded my recognition of social class differences. We were all Italians— some of us just had a little bit more money.

As Gertrude checked the address against her census worksheet, she would have noticed that the house at 412 had two separate entrances from a single front porch. The 412 Busti Avenue address was not a single-family home, although it resembled one to a casual observer. It had been a single-family structure before my grandfather, Benedetto Gardo, divided the house into two flats to provide rental income. Gertrude was alerted by the separate front entrances that the house actually contained two households; one could say it was a "vertical duplex," in contrast to a duplex with two households, side by side.

And there was also that second structure, the two-story cottage behind the first home – though still having the same address. It was not easily visible from the front of the house. It was only accessible from the street, through a narrow five-foot wide passage, between the closely spaced houses.

All of this was owned by my grandfather, whom I knew as "Nonno." What Gertrude learned on that visit was that at 412 Busti Avenue there were four households – in three of which the families were related.

Gertrude was most likely to have been professionally dressed, wearing a wool jacket over a blouse and a long skirt that extended to her calves.

---

6 Unfortunately, much of the park and all of the stables were replaced by the Niagara spur of the New York State Thruway (I-90) in the following decades. The highway was a true insult to the beauty of Front Park and the magnificent Lake Erie and Niagara River waterfront. The open space and natural beauty of the West Side were sacrificed to connect the Niagara spur to the I-90 Interstate system. Pedestrian access to the waterfront has been limited to a few over- and underpasses of the highway for several miles of Buffalo's waterfront.

This was the common uniform for middle-aged, middle-class women at the time. This was not the type of clothing worn by the women of Busti Avenue. There were no professional women living in this neighborhood in 1940.

The temperature on April 4th, the morning of the interview, had not quite reached 50°, which was typical spring weather in Buffalo. Angela Gardo, my grandmother – Nonna as I called her – was 55 years old and was at home as always. She wore a housedress, often covered by an apron, as did most immigrant Italian neighborhood women. The housedress – a patterned cotton dress which concealed the wearer's shape – was the uniform of that time and place. In the 14 years that my grandmother lived beyond the 1940 census, I do not recall her ever wearing a "formal" dress. The only knowledge I had of my grandmother being "dressed-up" was from a few old photos on display in the house. And she was, of course, well dressed at her wake in 1954.

Gertrude would have been wearing a U.S. Census identification badge that could have been misinterpreted by most immigrants (and certainly by my Nonna) as a "police" badge. Nonna would have watched suspiciously through the parlor window from behind lace curtains as Gertrude arrived at the front door. She surely would have asked herself, "Why is this woman coming to my house?" Angela could not imagine what she, her husband, or "Dio-Mio" (my God) one of her children could have done that would necessitate a visit by a government official. Angela would have called to her twenty-three-year-old daughter Rose to come to see the woman approaching the front porch. Gertrude would have then introduced herself to my grandmother and Aunt Rose. Angela did not speak English. Rose spoke both English and an Italian dialect.

Aunt Rose was surely followed closely by Angela when they opened the door for Gertrude. Gertrude listed the two – Angela and Rose – as both being respondents on the census form. Rose reported that Angela only spoke Italian – but that was not technically true. My Nonna actually spoke a Sicilian dialect, and even a person who spoke fluent Italian would have had difficulty understanding her.[7]

The Census report was based on information from two parallel conversations: one conversation would have been between Gertrude and Rose, and the other was between my grandmother and Rose, who then reported back to Gertrude. This arrangement would have continued until the census form had been completed.

Gertrude most likely started by saying, "Let's talk about the persons living in your household," but then continued the interview using the word *home* instead of household. Gertrude would have explained to Rose that household meant everyone who lived in a single flat or apartment, even unrelated persons. The data show that Gertrude reported family members in three separate households. This was my extended, intergenerational family, representing three generations.

The older generation were immigrants – this included my grandparents, my great- great-uncles, and my father, who were all born in Italy. My grandfather (Nonno) Benedetto Gardo emigrated to the United States from Sicily in 1907. His wife, my grandmother (Nonna), Angela, would scream in Italian at me – Vincenzo – from the front porch, "Mannaggia America." She was saying "Curse you America, you are stealing my grandson." She understood that the younger generations, including me, were different – and becoming more and more removed from her values. We were acquiring different "ideas," and there was very little she could do about it. Eventually, she haltingly and cautiously accepted some American values. My grandmother never learned to speak English.

---

7 Italy only became a single unified nation in 1871, and its separate languages and dialects were still prominent in the early 20th century, when my grandmother came to America. These languages and dialects are still common today, though the "Italian" language is somewhat more unified than it was 100 years ago (https://imageearthtravel.com/2019/06/30/italian-languages-dialects-hands/).

This photo appeared in The Buffalo Evening News circa 1915. My grandmother's brothers, Dominic and Sam Pilleteri, and my grandfather's brother Tom are all standing and circled in the photo. My grandfather, holding my uncle Russell, is seated and appears in the large circle; to his right (seated) is his brother Ignazio. The rest of the men pictured lived in our neighborhood.

The next generation included my mother and her siblings (my four aunts and two uncles) – all born in the United States. The women were pulled between a male-dominated "Old World" paternalism and the increasing number of social and economic opportunities that America provided.

Although they were the first generation born in America, they were largely influenced by Italian values. My mother was born one year after my grandmother arrived in the United States, and in a sense, she was never far removed from Sicily. My mother, the oldest of the first-generation Americans, had our nuclear family at the same 412 address where her entire family of origin lived. There was not much separation at all.

But there were important differences in the extent and speed of assimilation among family members. There was an 18-year age gap between my mother, the oldest Gardo, and her sister, Josephine, the youngest child.

This time span was reflected in the "intra-generational" differences in life-style choices among the seven children, especially for the women.

In 1940, my brother and I were the sole members of the third generation of this family – and the second generation of Americans. (I still joke, though, that I'm a "first -and-a-half generation" American, given that my father had emigrated from Italy.) My family spoke English at home, even though my father's first language was Italian. (And some of the English I learned on the streets I knew it was best not to bring home.) Speaking English was testimony to our desire to assimilate totally and quickly as Americans.

Angela would have continued to stay close to Rose during the entire interview, making certain the "correct" information was given in response to all questions. Angela's apparent "supervision" of the interview was not surprising – even though she would not have been able to understand the conversation between Rose and Gertrude. Did she remain a part of the interview session to exert parental authority over Rose by her mere presence, even though she did not know what was being said and definitely did not understand what was being written down on the Census form? Angela always wanted to be in charge of something she thought was important even if she didn't know what it was. Rose would not have known how to explain to Angela the purpose of the Census – but she did know that it was legally required.

Rose was an attractive woman, as were all the Gardo women. She had long, lustrous black hair and a dark, smooth olive complexion, which she thought was oily. Rose frequently dabbed her face with alcohol before she applied makeup. By today's standards, Rose would be considered an Italian beauty. Indeed, she had a striking resemblance to Dorothy Lamour, a popular 1940s Hollywood actress. Rose was keenly aware that her olive complexion marked her as not only Italian, but as a dark-complexioned Sicilian. She was always concerned with being identified as an uncultured Italian, and feared being thought of as lacking in class, manners and social grace. She was aware that Italians were not fully integrated into American middle-class society and culture. Rose strove hard all her life to be identified as an American and longed to be treated as modern, cultured, and refined.

Rose was considered pretentious and "uppity" by her brothers and sisters and her nieces and nephews – including me. As a youngster, I thought she was demanding, sometimes mean, and *always* bossy. She required that I behave "properly." As Rose grew older she did not continue to work in a factory as her sisters did. Rose found work as a clerk in high-end department stores, where she could dress up – and where she would not be considered an "ignorant factory girl." She enjoyed associating with middle-class women whom she considered to be cultured, even though she was only a clerk. What Rose wanted most was to be considered a cultured American woman.

So, Rose's role in the interaction with Gertrude was not surprising. What was surprising, though, was the information that was conveyed – or not conveyed. Angela's bachelor brother, my great-uncle Sam Pillitteri, was not reported to Gertrude. Great Uncle Sam was a World War I U.S. Army veteran and a U.S. citizen in 1940. He had lived with my grandparents since immigrating to America in 1911. Did Angela instruct Rose not to report Uncle Sam to Gertrude? Was my grandmother fearful about naming Uncle Sam since he wasn't one of her children? Why did they think it best not to report Uncle Sam? The rationale behind this decision went to the grave with Nonna (and with Aunt Rose).

After finishing the discussion with Nonna and Aunt Rose, Gertrude would have come to the house "in the back" – my house. Although we lived "downstairs," Gertrude still had to walk up a short flight of seven stairs to our front door, the one on the right; the door on the left led to a much longer flight of stairs that went to my great-uncle and aunt's flat. The outside landing was narrow and dangerous. Gertrude entered through the kitchen, the only entrance there was to my house; there was no hallway to soften the cold air that came in all winter, whenever the door was opened. Gertrude was met by my father and mother, who were home at the time. (My father was working the second shift that week, which started at 4 PM and ended at midnight— if he didn't work overtime.)

Gertrude introduced herself as the census taker and asked my parents with whom she was talking. Gertrude recorded those answers: my father identified himself as Joseph A. Marando and my mother said she was Grace Marando. My parents had become "respondents." All three would have sat at the kitchen table to conduct the interview.

The kitchen was the most-used room of our flat, which had two bedrooms, a living room (which we called the "parlor") and a bathroom. In reality, the kitchen was the "living room" as well. We did not have a dining room; we had all our meals at the kitchen table. There was a potbelly coal-fired stove in the kitchen that heated the house during the winter. I remember the stove quite well. One day I put a paper bag over my head and danced around the kitchen bumping into the hot stove. I was not burned, but I was quite frightened. My father put me into his lap to comfort me, which I enjoyed.

I suspect my mother took the lead in answering Gertrude's questions; she usually took the lead in all conversations. I can picture my father adding commentary and offering details to questions, as he usually did. He thought more carefully than my mother and was good at remembering details.

My mother indicated that there were four Marando family members. My father Joseph (he indicated that his "given" name was Giuseppe) was born in Italy on May 19, 1909. My mother Grace was born July 29, 1911 in Buffalo. (To all her friends, neighbors and kids she declared she was born a year later, in 1912. It was not unusual for the Gardo children, especially the women, to "shave" a year or two off their birth year. I did not know my mother was born in 1911 until I saw her death certificate in 1984.) I was identified as the oldest son, Vincent, born August 25, 1938 and named after my paternal grandfather in Italy, whom I never met. Benjamin, the second son, was born 14 months later on November 3, 1939. My brother should have been named Benedict, the English translation for Benedetto, after my maternal grandfather. At the hospital when Benny was born, a nurse asked my mother what to name him, my mother said Benny – so the nurse put down Benjamin.

Benny (left) and I, circa 1943-44.

Given that my father had been born in Italy, Gertrude recorded him as an Alien (AL) – but not as an "undocumented alien" as he might have been recorded in a later census. My father entered the United States in 1929 illegally at New York City (an official port of entry). He did not become a

US citizen until 1949, after World War II. "Joe" as he was called by all – except us kids – was born in the southern most mainland province of Italy – Calabria. "Joe" and three teenaged boys from his village of Gioiosa Iconica boarded a ship at Reggio, Calabria for their "indirect" route to the United States. There is no documentation of his passage to the United States. The four young men (really teenagers) traveled first to Buenos Aires, Argentina where they resided for a year before making the second leg of their journey to the United States. The route they chose to the United States from Italy – via Argentina – was very strategic. Traveling to Argentina first and then on to the United States was a prudent choice for escaping detection. Traveling directly to the United States from Italy would have increased the probability of their being caught by US immigration officials as illegal immigrants bypassing Ellis Island.

For Italians, legal entrance to the United States in the late 1920s was quite limited. Only about 5,000 Italians per year were allowed into the country under the terms of the United States Immigration Act of 1924. This legislation limited persons from southern and Eastern Europe in accordance with the number of people from their nation of origin who resided in the United States in 1890. Few southern and Eastern Europeans resided in the United States at that time, so in 1924 these populations were limited in their ability to legally immigrate to the United States. (We often forget this, but discrimination toward immigrants from particular countries is not just a recent phenomenon.)

When the ship from Argentina arrived in the New York Harbor, the four Italian teenagers paid a bribe to some of the ship's crew to overlook their dis-embarkment. All four boys had relatives in the New York City area who provided them with shelter and contacts for obtaining work. If the four boys had arrived in the United States today, they would be classified as undocumented or illegal immigrants. [8]

After noting my father's status as an immigrant, Gertrude recorded his occupation as a laborer, employed by the New York Central Railroad Freight House. His 1939 yearly earnings were recorded as $875, which was close to the national median income of $954. The freight house also employed my grandfather as a supervisor, more accurately as a "work gang boss." I suspect my grandfather Gardo had arranged a job for my father at the freight house.[9]

Interestingly, the situation changed shortly after Gertrude's visit. In 1941 my father secured a job (and a raise) at the Buffalo Flour Mills before the United States entered the Second World War. Again, my father was helped, getting this job through a relative. My Uncle Ignazio, who worked at the flour mill for decades, made the contact that resulted in my father's employment. As a major industrial center, Buffalo had gone into full wartime production by 1941.

My father kept that job for 10 years until the Buffalo Flour Mills Corporation left Buffalo in 1951 due to a decline in business and labor-management issues. My father was offered an opportunity to relocate with the Corporation to its headquarters in Minneapolis, Minnesota. But moving to Minneapolis was not an option for my mother; there was no alternative for her to remain with the Gardos – her family of origin, her extended family. My parents would live their entire lives in Buffalo.

---

8 The derogatory term "wetback" has been used to describe Mexican immigrants illegally crossing the Rio Grande River to come to the United States; I have been known to say that in a manner of speaking, my father and his friends were "wetbacks" even though they didn't get wet. I don't intend any disrespect by my use of this term – my intention is merely to highlight that illegal immigration has been taking place for quite some time and hasn't really changed much even though we now seek to demean some illegal immigrants by labeling them. The bottom line for me is this: without illegal immigration I probably wouldn't be here. When I say my father and his friends were "wetbacks without getting wet," I am expressing solidarity with those in the Mexican community who have had to live with this label, knowing that if such a term had existed in the 1940s, my family and I would have been similarly labeled.
9 This was a common pattern of finding employment for immigrants at that time, and it continues to the present day.

Our 1940 rent was reported as $18 per month for the downstairs four-room flat in the back. The $18 rent was a moderate percentage of our income when compared to today's rents – and this contrast is especially stark when we think about the percentage of income rent takes up for most laborers today. Of course, my grandfather may have given my parents a break of a few dollars on the monthly rent; though after comparing other neighborhood rents, $18 was not substantially different than what others in the neighborhood were paying.[10]

My mother, Grace (Gaetana on her birth certificate) was recorded in the census as 28 years old. (After my mother was given the name Grace by her first-grade teacher, she was forevermore referred to as Grace.) Her occupation was recorded as "homemaker" and remained so her entire life.

That "homemaker" designation says so little. My mother was a fantastic cook; in contemporary terms, she might even be termed a "gourmet chef." She turned inexpensive, ordinary foods into culinary masterpieces. During World War II fine cuts of meat and other food items such as sugar were rationed, scarce or expensive. She would take low-end cuts of organ meat such as kidneys, liver, and brains (sweetbreads) and create meals that were the match of any served in Buffalo's finest restaurants. Our family always ate well; we were the envy of relatives, friends and neighbors.

My mother was gregarious and outgoing. She was a lively soul who enjoyed socializing and entertaining. She had many "girl" friends and belonged to several social groups. She would often say "I am going to my 'club' tonight" as she left us kids with a babysitter. Her gregariousness and love of a good time was in contrast to my father's quiet and often solemn nature. He was not humorous and did not often laugh or smile. He had few male friends. He socialized very little, and when he did, it was exclusively among relatives.

My mother sacrificed greatly on behalf of me and all her children. She often subjugated her outgoing personality for the well-being of her

---

10 Per 1940 Census data for the area.

family. As I grew older, she and I often disagreed. At times I wasn't sure she knew what she was talking about, or what she was doing. Yet, her heart was always open; she forgave my transgressions, both big and small. Like her, I was often loud and not mindful of how I affected those around me. She was assertive (possibly bossy and nosey) and did not hesitate to share her opinions with others and about others. She always meant well. My mother was charismatic; few persons would forget her after getting to know her.

She was also the family disciplinarian. She was often not informed by family members and relatives of my poor behavior; some relatives were concerned that she would spank me. In particular, my Great Aunt Rosalia, living upstairs, did not feel a spanking was necessary or warranted for what I did. Most of the time, I was self-disciplined, knowing anything that I wasn't supposed to do in the family compound would be noticed. Someone "might" tell my mother and she would hit me. My father never spanked me; he was usually at work and rarely at home during the day to see how I behaved. Even if he was at home, he would not spank me – though some-times he would "holler" at me.

Gertrude recorded Benny and me as the only Marando children in 1940. We were close not only in age—14 months, but in what we did together— at least at first. My mother expected me to take care of Benny. I felt a responsibility for seeing that he did not get into trouble. He followed me everywhere when we were outside, at least at the beginning. Then he quickly made up his own mind and rarely listened to me. Benny was inquisitive and from my perspective, he was always getting into harmless and often humorous mischief.

My mother's instructions that he listen to me were usually for naught; after all, I wasn't going to be a "tattle tale" and report him to my parents. I felt that he could get away with things for which I would have been held to account. One day he opened a can of paint in the cellar and painted the legs of the wringer washing machine. At that time washing machines had wringers to squeeze the water out of clothes before hanging them up to further dry. (There were no electric clothes dryers at that time.)

When my mother saw what Benny had done to the washing machine, she thought it was funny and laughed. Her remark was that it was "only Benny." I was expected to be much more mature. I did not bother to rebel at the expectation of my being responsible for Benny. My parents didn't back me up in disciplining Benny, so why should he listen to me? And why should I really care?

Benny was very athletic and soon was able to run faster than me. I was not able to catch him when he ran away from me. In high school he became the city's premier quarterback and was a Buffalo All-High School selection during his junior and senior years of high school. He also led the city All-Star city team against the county All-Star team in their annual game.

Benny during his senior year of high school (circa 1958).

I did not want Benny to hang around me and my friends when play-ing outdoors. I also escaped from him when I went to my grandparent's house in the "front," or climbed upstairs to my Uncle Ignazio and Aunt's Rosalia's house.

When she had finished recording all of us, Gertrude thanked my father and mother for inviting her into the kitchen and responding to the census. As Gertrude was leaving our house to interview the upstairs household, she may have remarked that she saw five-month-old Benjamin in his crib, but did not see or hear Vincent. My mother would have responded, "Vinnie is not here, he is in the hospital being treated for polio. We don't know when he'll be home. We are not sure he will be able to walk when he comes home."

Gertrude had taken the count of our "household" – a very different kind of household than most Americans live in today, as the 2020 census was recently taken. We were three households at one address, most of us related, and a couple of us missing – either from the count or from the home. I'll never know why Uncle Sam was overlooked. But my young self was in the midst of that era's public health crisis: polio, a disease which primarily affected the children of my generation and would have impacts that rippled out through the United States over the next several decades, and into the 21st century in several developing countries.

CHAPTER 2:

POLIO

When Gertrude Bunce visited 412 Busti Avenue to conduct the 1940 census, I wasn't at home. I was in a hospital recuperating from polio, as my parents often brought to my attention when I was older. I was hospitalized in September 1939, when I was 13 months old; I did not return home for a year. Few official records exist of my contracting polio, and only pieces of conversations that took place over the course of decades support my understanding of my yearlong hospital and convalescence period.

To be clear, the lack of information and my knowledge of only fragments about the earliest circumstances of my polio make this retelling a bit unusual. I have no conscious memory of what I have written concerning my experience with actually having polio.

I believe my parents used the term a "year" loosely as the time of my absence. I may have been away 10 months, 12 months or possibly a while longer. I have not been able to uncover any historical documentation of my hospitalization or rehabilitation treatment. With the exception of my Aunt Josephine who was 12 years old at the time, all other adult family members who might have been able to describe my treatment have died. Josephine died in March 2020 as I was preparing this manuscript.

When I contracted polio (poliomyelitis) in 1939, it was the most-feared disease in the United States. At that time, polio was a disease without a cure and still has no cure. How the disease spread was not understood by the medical profession and so, of course, it was also a mystery to the public. Once a person contracted the disease its damage was permanent. The effects were primarily paralysis of the limbs (particularly the legs), and deformity often accompanied this paralysis. Prevention was not really possible until the mid-1950s when a vaccine was formulated by Dr. Jonas Salk. The vaccine was highly effective in immunizing individuals against the disease. At that point, the once-feared disease was prevented and that was the end of its conquest in the United States. Polio began slipping into U.S. history.

But on that day in 1940 when Gertrude knocked on our door, there was no preventative, there was no cure – there was just me with polio, eighteen months old and living in a hospital away from my family. Reviewing the 1940 U. S. Census stimulated my thinking about the effects of polio – and gave me a new perspective on the year I spent in the hospital, a little boy separated from my family. I had given casual thought to the effect polio had on me and my family over the decades, but I've come to understand that the results of that time – that treatment, that separation – it was all incredibly important.

Since Jonas Salk's vaccine was introduced to the U.S. in 1955, polio has become a historical phenomenon: cases had dropped dramatically by the mid-1960s, and the last case of polio in the U.S. was recorded in 1979. (Indeed, polio has been nearly eradicated worldwide; only 95 cases were reported in 2019.[11]) As this disease has essentially been relegated to the dustbins of history, few people now understand what it was and why it caused such panic.

Polio resulted in several forms of paralysis in addition to the limbs. A more severe form of paralysis affected muscles controlling an individual's

11 It would be possible to completely eradicate polio if there was not fear of the vaccine, particularly in remote areas of some developing countries. Atul Gawande presents a compelling discussion of this issue in his book *Better* (New York: Henry Holt & Co., 2007).

breathing. This form of the disease was known as *Bulbar polio*; Bulbar patients were unable to breathe on their own. Individuals who had contracted Bulbar polio needed the assistance of a mechanical device to breathe. The device often shown in photos and at the movies was referred to as an "Iron Lung." It was a tubular machine in which patients lay prone and immobile and mechanical power was applied to their diaphragm/lungs to assist them in inhaling and exhaling. The lifespan of Bulbar patients was generally greatly shortened. Most children who contracted Bulbar polio did not reach adulthood.[12] Images of the Iron Lung in newspapers or shown in newsreels at movie theaters or on TV provoked additional fear with the public, even though this form of polio only occurred in about 2% of cases of persons being affected.

Polio struck children under five years old in a disproportionately high percentage of all cases. As a result of this, polio was often referred to as "infantile paralysis." Facing paralysis and possible death added to most peoples' apprehension and fear of having children attend large group activities – where the disease was thought to spread. The highest incidences of polio occurred during the warmer summer months. There was "suspicion" by the medical profession that large crowds, often at swimming pools, facilitated the spread of polio. Swimming pools were often closed due to fear of contracting the polio virus. September school openings were delayed until the incidence of the disease lessened with the advent of cooler weather. As temperatures dropped, the spread of the disease diminished until the following year, when the weather became warmer during the spring summer and groups once again congregated – and the number of cases of polio rose.

How the virus was spread within a population was not known in 1939, when I contracted the disease. At that time, there was an assumption within the medical profession and reported by the media that dirt and grime lay at the root of the spread of the virus, but the precise conditions

---

12 A shortened lifespan was likely, though not guaranteed; there are currently reports of a 75-year-old polio survivor who still relies on an iron lung in 2021 (https://en.wikipedia.org/wiki/Paul_Alexander_(lawyer).

that spread the disease were not fully known. Some thought that spread occurred through coming into contact with individuals who carried the virus – but 70% of persons carrying the polio virus exhibited no symptoms. Increased knowledge and awareness of how the disease spread did not eliminate or lessen the spread of the disease in the decade and a half after I contracted polio; it was only the development of a vaccine that brought the epidemic to a halt.

Later research found that the cause for the spread of the disease was through a victim's ingestion of infected fecal matter. The polio virus attacked the nervous system through the digestive system. The virus affected the spine and often the nerves in the legs, the arms, also the back and chest.

Polio was never the leading cause of death by a disease, either in the U.S. or worldwide. The number of Americans that contracted polio during the entire first half of the 20th century was significantly less than 1 million persons; the highest number of reported cases of polio in the nation was 57,000 cases in 1952. Death from influenza far exceeded that from polio; the 1918-19 influenza epidemic was the cause of death for more than a million Americans (and tens of millions of individuals worldwide).

A primary difference between influenza and polio, however, was that the cause of influenza was known. Effective prevention could be medically pursued; the effects of influenza could be effectively monitored by scientists and treated with a "flu" vaccine – so the incidence of illness and death could be reduced. In contrast, the uncertain cause of polio, there being no known cure – and the probability of paralysis – fueled mass hysteria.

Polio was the first disease to be communicated nationally by modern mass media technology: radio, motion pictures and television. Televised fundraising telethons highlighted the disease in an effort to battle polio and infantile paralysis. Well-known entertainers, such as Jerry Lewis, introduced celebrities to involve the public in soliciting contributions to combat the disease.

I was identified as having contracted polio by street address, not by name, in an official 1939 Buffalo Health Department document.[13] There were 347 Buffalo residents who contracted polio in 1939, and all of us were reported in the Fronczak Report. Most victims were young children: of the 347 polio cases reported in Buffalo that year, 284 children were under ten and a half years old. Of the children, 37 were young children, less than two and half years old — including me. This was a verification of the term "infantile paralysis."

In the Commissioner's report, I was identified as case number 268: a 1 ½-year-old male living at 412 Busti Avenue. I have not found my name in any official document as having contracted polio. Polio cases were cited as an epidemic by The Buffalo Evening News, which tracked the incidence of polio and reported most cases, but not all. The cases were cited in the newspaper to inform and alert the public about the extent of the disease. Newspaper reports offered encouraging descriptions of progress made in the decreasing numbers as of the Fall of 1939. I assume newspaper reports were written to soothe the public's fears by highlighting a decrease in the number of polio cases.[14]

---

13 *The Outbreak of Poliomyelitis*, City of Buffalo 1939, Francis E. Fronczak, M.D. D. Sc. P.H., Commissioner of Health; Frank R. Whelply, M.D. and Alfred E. Regan, M.D., Division of Communicable Disease.

14 In contrast to the 1939 polio epidemic, the U.S. Centers of Disease Control and Prevention (CDC) reported in 2018 that a polio-like disease, Acute Flaccid Myelitis (AFM) was present in the country. Similar to polio, AFM struck mostly young children, many of whom suffered paralysis. The CDC identified less than 500 cases across 36 states between 2012-2018 as an epidemic. Similar to polio, AFM strikes mostly young children, many of whom suffer paralysis. The severity of Buffalo's 1939 polio epidemic of 347 cases is massive compared to the number of cases of AFM found nationwide over a six-year period. Of course, the 347 cases is itself quite small compared to the number of cases of Covid-19 in its first year of existence in the U.S. (almost 25 million at the one year anniversary of the disease's U.S. appearance in January 2021).

Me as a baby, sometime before being diagnosed with polio.

Symptoms of polio were first noticed by my 17-year-old godmother, Mary Gardo – my mother's sister. I was told that as Aunt Mary was drying me on the kitchen table after a bath, she noticed that that I leaned to my left side as she held me. Aunt Mary observed that I favored my left leg and did not extend my right leg to the table. I was told that Aunt Mary said, "Grace, you should come over and look at Vinnie's leg." My mother and Aunt Mary looked me over. They discussed how my right foot did not extended to the floor when they held me. My mother and aunt also held me up at arm's length with my legs dangling in the air. They further realized that I did not kick my legs with equal force; the right leg curled up. At 13 months I had not yet learned to walk. They knew no real test of leg strength, or of my ability to walk. The two women discussed their observations and wondered out loud, "what could that mean?" They had no way to grasp the full meaning of their "tests."

The observations of my aunt and mother were the first recognition of my possibly having contracted polio. In all the following years there was never any mention of my having any other recognizable symptoms, such as fever, headache and/or stiff neck prior to paralysis, which commonly accompanied the acute onset stage of polio.[15] I was too young to identify any pain. If I expressed any discomfort or pain prior to when they noticed my leg, the cause was not recognized as polio. I may have been past the acute stage of polio before the official medical diagnosis in September 1939.

According to my aunt, she and my mother discussed bringing me to visit a trusted nearby Italian druggist, as the first step in getting an "expert" to examine me. They felt that the pharmacist would advise them about to what to do, if anything. The next day my parents went to see this local pharmacist to express their concerns about me possibly having polio. They asked him what he thought about my favoring the left leg. According to my Aunt Josephine, my mother put me up on the drugstore counter to show the pharmacist my legs. Upon observing me, the pharmacist said that my case could be serious. I should be seen by a doctor – soon. Dr. Frank K. Potts, an orthopedic surgeon, became my primary physician.

This is the Italian pharmacy my mother and my Aunt Josephine brought me to after they realized something was wrong with my legs. Photo: Buffalo Historical Society.

---

15 Daniel Wilson's 2007 book, *Living with Polio: The Epidemic and Its Survivors* (University of Chicago Press), details the progression of disease and its aftermath by interviewing over 100 people who had contracted the disease between 1930 and 1960.

Dr. Potts had a private practice and was a faculty member at the University of Buffalo Medical School, Department of Orthopedics. Dr. Potts officially identified and confirmed that I had contracted polio on September 28, 1939 as reported by the Buffalo Health Commissioner. Upon Dr. Potts' diagnosis, I was immediately hospitalized.

I assume that I was put into isolation and quarantined, so as not to spread the disease. The accepted method of treatment in 1939 was immobilization of the affected limbs. Patients were put into splints or braces and kept immobile so that they would not strain their muscles. The accepted medical thinking and practice at the time was that muscles needed to be relaxed and not subjected to fatigue. Rest was required.

My mother said I wore braces while in the hospital. Reports in the literature of polio patients at this time reveal that braces, splints, and in some cases plaster casts, kept legs immobile. Yet braces are commonly associated with patients standing or attempting to walk. I did not walk when I entered the hospital. I don't know when I started to walk. Walking was never discussed.

My not having been able to walk upon entering the hospital may have posed a dilemma for the attending physicians. The primary reason I did not walk when entering the hospital was my age. At 13 months, I had not yet learned to walk. The effect of polio on whether I could walk or not must have been puzzling to the doctors who cared for me. Was my not being able to walk a function of polio, or of age? If walking was a test of the full extent of polio's effects on me, then medical professionals had to wait until they were certain that it was not the disease that had affected my ability to walk. That test was most likely verified after some time, possibly a year.

When I was first admitted to the hospital, in September of 1939, I was unable to distinguish between any of my feelings: I couldn't tell my caregivers whether I was in physical pain, emotional discomfort, hungry, fearful because I was separated from my family, or experiencing any other specific emotion. I suspect the doctors took sufficient time and proceeded cautiously in diagnosing the reasons for my immobility. I was a big baby and less likely to walk early (smaller, more agile children tended to walk earlier). Most likely not walking and not talking were circumstances that my caregivers had to take into consideration before fully assessing the damaging effects of polio upon me.

I believe that toward the end of a year's stay in the hospital I was able to pull myself up to a standing position in a crib. The ability to stand may have been a critical signal as to the extent of polio's impact upon me. If I could stand, I might be able to walk. It seemed to take that full year to identify and sort out the reasons for my limited mobility. The limited extent of the physical effects of polio on me were verified when I walked and being able to walk was the "proof" required so I could be released. With polio damage limited to one leg, and since I could walk, I was considered "cured." When I was "cured" and released, all were pleased – especially my parents.

How I contracted polio was never really determined. A common assumption in 1939 was that dirt and unclean environments contributed to – if they were not the cause of – contracting polio. The science of identifying the underlying causes of polio and the factors that enhanced its spread was not sophisticated at that time. Many potential sources for contracting and spreading the disease were assumed or hypothesized by the medical profession, but there was little definitive knowledge. It would be another decade and a half before science fully put an end to the disease in the United States.

Speculation accompanied the Buffalo medical community's investigative efforts to grasp causes of the polio epidemic in 1939. The Buffalo Commissioner of Health, assisted by the New York State Department of Health epidemiologist's investigation of polio, examined all Buffalo polio victims and their households [Fronczak report]. Interspersed and underlying their explanation of cause was the identification of some form of unsanitary environment surrounding most victims. Dirt and filth were constant factors the medical community reported to be associated with contracting the disease. The report confirmed that a lack of cleanliness and/or poor hygiene habits were necessary or accompanying conditions for contracting polio. Dirt and unsanitary conditions were considered to facilitate polio's spread among an unclean population.

Unclean environments often associated with lower class populations – especially immigrants – were considered by some in the medical profession to be a contributing, if not the causal, factor for contracting polio. Indeed, this was the stated assumption of the 1939 Buffalo Health Commissioner's report.

The 1939 Buffalo Health Commissioner's report insinuated that particular among "dirty" immigrants in catching polio were the Italians, more precisely the Sicilians who inhabited Buffalo's West Side. Implied in the findings was that Italians were unsanitary and more susceptible to contracting polio than other immigrant groups and certainly more so than Anglo-Americans. Not acknowledged, in 1939, was that middle-class residents – often suburbanites – also contracted polio. The link between polio and middle-class (and even upper middle-class) non-immigrants should have been evident, even at that time in the unfolding spread of the disease. A decade and a half later, subsequent advances in medical science and research found the relationship between dirt and polio to be more nuanced and less direct than was thought in 1939.

I am certain my parents felt a responsibility, if not shame and guilt, for why I contracted the disease. How I contracted polio was not generally discussed in my presence, though I knew my parents were mystified about how I had gotten sick. My mother came to believe that my contracting polio was a "curse" for some prior evil deed on her and my father's part. She said that they broke a rental lease with a nearby landlord so they could move to my grandfather's rental flat. That curse was the root cause of my polio, as far as my mother was concerned.

I assume I was first taken to Buffalo Children's Hospital, two miles from my home. When doctors determined that the polio had subsided, and I was no longer contagious, I was most likely transferred from the hospital to the Josephine Goodyear Home for Disabled Children in suburban Williamsville, eight miles from my home. Many children received therapy for polio at The Josephine Goodyear Home, and I believe that I was one of the children treated at the facility – though there are no written records, and the facility no longer exists (it was no longer needed after polio was eliminated). I assume I received physical therapy and physical rehabilitation for a portion of my "hospital "stay.

I say this because my parents said that the "hospital" was far away and there were no buses to get there. For that year that I was in the "hospital," my parents needed a car to be able to visit me. Eight miles was quite a distance at that time without owning, or having access to, an auto – and my parents did not own an automobile and they did not know how to drive. My parents were limited to inconvenient public transportation or dependent on relatives to reach wherever I was being cared for – especially if I was in suburban Williamsville as I believe. Either my grandfather, or one of my uncles (Buddy or Russell), had to drive my parents to visit me.

I was told that I was excited when my parents and relatives visited. They said that I screamed when I saw them and demanded to be served my meals before other child patients. (My demand to be served first suggests that I was in a ward of many children.) What was not discussed by my family was my disposition or demeanor when they left, not to return to again for a week or more. Research suggests that in that era hospitals had limited visiting hours and tightly controlled the information on the prognosis of the disease provided to parents.

Visiting the hospital was a burden for both my mother and my father. When I was first hospitalized, my mother was seven months pregnant with my brother Benjamin (Benny) who was born on November 3, 1939. After his birth, my mother would have had to take my infant brother with her to the hospital to visit me – or she would have had to get someone to care for my brother if she came to visit me alone. My mother had her hands full with a newborn child who needed constant attention and care. My father worked long hours and was only free on Sundays; he often worked as a laborer on the 4PM to 12AM shift or the midnight to 8 AM shift at the New York Central Freight House and was unable to accompany my mother on hospital visits except on Sundays.

On top of the challenges of transportation, there was also the issue of finances. Statistical data indicate that the cost of a year's hospital stay in 1940 was approximately $1000, depending on the type of illness. This amount was more than my father's reported 1939 annual income of $875. I do not know how or who paid for my hospital stay, medical care and therapy, but I do know that there was no way my family could have afforded the hospital and therapy costs. Family contributions, charity and public assistance must have been the sources for payment of care.

I heard my parents say that some very wealthy people helped them buy needed medical items, such as a crib, leg braces, bedding, and orthopedic shoes. I suspect that the "wealthy people" were associated either with the March of Dimes organization or with the Josephine Goodyear Foundation. Unfortunately, no one will ever really know: when I contacted each organization, I was told that no documents related to my case were available.

When I returned home from the hospital as a two-year-old, I was able to walk without braces. I may have also learned to talk under the care of nurses, doctors and health personnel while I was in an institutional setting.

While I was in the hospital, I am certain I learned to pay attention to adults. Getting attention from professional staff was a key to my comfort, if not my well-being. I may have learned to speak and communicate with adults during my year in treatment. I needed to get attention from the staff. Getting attention took effort. I must have watched adult caretakers closely as to how to get them to respond to my calls for assistance and companionship.

The skills of paying attention and being able to get a response are what I brought home when I returned. I was fortunate that I had constant support with my grandparents, aunts and uncles all living at the same address. They all treated me as a special child.

The home I returned was different than when I left the year before, and this was not necessarily due to the effects of polio. I was no longer an only child; I now had a brother. Upon returning home I was treated with special care as a polio victim by some relatives and neighbors, although I never considered myself disabled. My Great Uncle Ignazio, who lived upstairs from me, would put me on his shoulders to go for a walk, when I could have walked on my own. I am certain he thought he was helping me. I liked to be carried, particularly on the shoulders of this very strong uncle, of whom I was quite fond.

I had been away from home during a critical stage of my childhood development – I had begun to walk and talk. It seems reasonable to me now that I wouldn't have any memory of my hospital stay or anything else – I was not even two years old. And because I was so young, the potentially dramatic effects of polio on me may have been minimal. But I have to admit that I'm not sure about that.

My parents never told me not to discuss polio – but my parents and relatives did not know how to express themselves concerning my polio. No one wanted to bring to my attention or remind me of the effect polio had on me. There were few family conversations of any kind – and that included any talk about polio – that might bring discomfort to my parents or to me. I was "cured" and the matter of how I had gotten sick was not brought up at home or elsewhere. I could walk, unaided, with only a slight limp. I could also run.

What continues to puzzle me, eight decades later, is that I did not question or even inquire about the circumstances of my hospitalization, rehabilitation, and therapy. Throughout my childhood – and even much of my adult life – I never reflected on the significance or impact that a year's "hospital" stay may have had upon me as a one-year-old. I suspect the separation from family may have had as much impact upon me as did the physical effects of polio.

Not until I started to write this reflection on my past did I begin to grasp the importance of my time away from my family and the lasting effects polio has had on me. The physical effects of the disease were moderate. Having had polio did not exclude me from playing any type of game with other children. I had to work harder than other children, but I usually stayed among the pack during outdoor play.

But I have realized that one important effect polio had on me was as a result of the prolonged separation from family when hospitalized for a year. While this was not a total separation (my parents and relatives did visit me), I have come to believe that the separation had a substantial impact on me. Recognizing the importance of this separation helps me to better understand my exceptional need to get attention, be recognized, and listened to by others. And as I write about the first eight years of my life, living on Busti Avenue, I felt I belonged there. I did not want to be separated from my extended family. I did not want to leave my home, again.[16]

Benny (right) and I, circa 1941. Note the difference in size between my right and left legs. This picture was probably taken shortly after I returned home from being in the hospital.

16 The 2018-19 Federal Administration's debacle of separating immigrant children from their family at the United States-Mexican border has weighed heavily on me as I reflected on my separation due to polio. Newspapers and electronic media have repeatedly reported on the consequences of the separations upon the young children.

For a time, until I was five years old, I wore special orthopedic shoes. The shoes were high-top with laces and metal islets around which I looped the laces. The orthopedic shoe store was quite a distance from home and difficult to reach without an automobile. The orthopedic shoes cost more than regular shoes. After reaching five years old I no longer wore the orthopedic shoes. I remember being quite happy not to wear the shoes anymore – although my "regular" shoes were always too narrow and at times they hurt. But I did not complain because I didn't want to go back to orthopedic high-top shoes.[17]

So I was home, and I was cured, and that was that. However, in the neighborhood my polio must've been discussed. When I was six, I engaged in a flailing scuffle with another boy, Louie, who was a year older than I. Louie was getting the better of me as we wrestled and pushed one another about until he immediately stopped fighting, as if I had somehow gotten the better of him. But I hadn't hurt him – he just stopped fighting. The next day I was told by a boy who watched the scuffle that Louie's father had broken up the fight by kicking his son in the shins. Louie's father had scolded him for fighting with me. Louie's father told his son that I had had polio and he should not fight with me again, because I could be easily injured.

Of course, I was not the only person that people in my life were aware of who had had polio. I had two heroes who were associated with polio. The first of these was President Franklin Delano Roosevelt (FDR). Knowledge of FDR's bout with polio in 1921 – two decades earlier than my case – was widely known. After all, he was the President of the United States. Roosevelt had contracted polio during the summer while on vacation at Campobello, Canada and could not walk unaided from then on.

There are few photos of President Roosevelt in a wheelchair during his campaigns for Governor of New York and for President of The United

---

17 Having shoes fit properly has been a lifelong problem. My feet are not the same size: currently my left foot size is 9G and my right foot is 8 ½ H. (The G and the H would translate into a 7E or an 8E by the common method of measuring shoe widths.) Indeed, shoe comfort has always been a top priority of mine. The type and quality of shoe have always been less important to me than the fit.

States. President Roosevelt was propped up against the podium when giving a speech, so he would have the appearance of standing on his own.

This continued throughout his four terms as the President: few photos revealed his inability to walk or stand. He was not often photographed sitting in a wheelchair; if he was, his legs were covered by a shawl or blanket. Most photos of President Roosevelt were of him sitting at a desk or riding seated in an automobile.

President Roosevelt's polio was not a secret – but it was not publicized or widely discussed. I'm not aware of any newspaper articles or any other commentary on the extent of the president's disability at that time. The media accommodated the President and his Administration's desire to not report the full limitations of his disability while he was carrying out the duties of the presidency.

Given that there was much discrimination against individuals with physical disabilities in the 1920s, 1930s, and 1940s, Franklin Delano Roosevelt's rise to the office of President of the United States in 1933 is all the more remarkable. Polio did not hinder him from being considered among the three "greatest" presidents -- George Washington, Abraham Lincoln and Franklin Delano Roosevelt-- by most scholars, myself included.

My other hero was the Australian nurse, Sister Elizabeth Kenny.[18] Sister Kenny raised skepticism and questioned the existing medical treatments that were being employed during the era when I had polio. She challenged the existing physical therapy techniques used at that time and advocated a different approach – which became known as the Kenny Method. At that time, the established local community protocols recommended that patients rest and often required immobilization to limit pain and muscle damage. Sister Kenny recommended that hot packs be applied to patients and that extremities and other areas affected by polio

---

18 The title Sister is used in Australia in reference to a nurse. It is not a religious title as it is in the United States. Sister Kenny's story was made into a movie starring Rosalind Russell in 1946.

be massaged – and most medical professionals at the time questioned her methods.[19]

But despite resistance, the medical profession eventually adopted the therapy techniques recommended by Sister Kenny. She was proven to be correct in her methods. The new physical therapy techniques were adopted after I was released from medical care in 1940.

Sister Kenny was also my mother's hero. My mother took me to meet Sister Kenny at a gathering in Buffalo in the mid-1940s, although unfortunately I have no memory of the visit. The fact that I could walk when we visited Sister Kenny was sufficient proof that I was cured. My mother was proud to meet Sister Kenny and proud to show me off as having received good care. I believe my mother wanted recognition by Sister Kennedy that I was indeed cured, with no apparent paralysis.

In re-examining Sister Kenny's contribution to treating polio patients, I am all the more impressed with her accomplishments. Given the discrimination and resistance she encountered, her tenacity was not only impressive, it was required. In the America of the 1940s, she was considered suspect, if not a "quack", not only because she was not a doctor; she was a woman, and an Australian – a foreigner. As a non-MD she successfully challenged the existing medical protocols for physical therapy. Many in the medical profession initially considered her a medical imposter. But it was *her* approach to the treatment of polio that eventually prevailed.

Our visit with Sister Kenny closed the door on my having had polio. I was considered "fully recovered," which was OK with me. I had a lot of things to do.

---

19 In her book *Polio Wars: Sister Kenny and the Golden Age of American Medicine* (Oxford University Press, 2013), Naomi Rogers discusses the historical aspects of the polio epidemic and the incredible work done (particularly by Sister Kenny) in pioneering treatment.

CHAPTER 3:

I HAD A VILLAGE

In 1996 – over five decades after Gertrude visited my home on Busti Avenue – then-First Lady Hillary Clinton authored a book entitled *It Takes a Village*. In it, she expounded on the African proverb that suggested that children did not just need parents, but rather were best off when they were able to interact with a range of adults – a whole village. I lived in a village, a whole Italian village – and almost all the members of this dynamic community lived at the same address. My village was my family and my neighborhood.

Gertrude had already spoken to the family/village matriarch, and then had come to speak to her eldest child – my mother. When Gertrude finished asking questions at our home, she thanked my father and mother, and then asked who lived upstairs. My mother said her Uncle Ignazio and Aunt Rosalia lived there. I assume my mother knew her aunt was home because they often had coffee together in the morning.

Gertrude then rang the bell to the upstairs flat, which was similar to ours, but much neater. Great Uncle Ignazio (Ignatius), my grandfather's brother, and his wife Rosalia lived there; he was 46 years old in 1940 and she was 35 – but she looked and acted much older. She was an American citizen, born in New York in 1905, and she spoke English. I did not realize she was a U.S. citizen until I read the 1940 Census in 2012.

Uncle Ignazio and Aunt Rosalia were childless when they answered Gertrude's census questions, and they remained so throughout their lives. They treated me as their child. I had constant access to their home and was a welcomed dinner guest almost every evening, except when my mother would say don't go upstairs and bother them. I never felt that I bothered them. If I hadn't been wanted, they would have asked me to go home. They never did.

I was always on good behavior when I was at Uncle Ignazio's and Aunt Rosalia's home. A gentle reminder was sufficient to alert me of something I shouldn't have said or done. My Aunt Rosalia would end her "reminder" with "if your mother only knew what you said." There were cracks in family communication and gaps in the lines of authority for me to crawl through. Very little information about my misbehaviors ever reached my parents, particularly from my Uncle and Aunt living upstairs.

One of the family stories I heard about my Uncle Ignazio and Aunt Rosalia was that they had asked my grandmother if they could adopt my Aunt Josephine. Josephine was the youngest of my grandmother's seven children – 18 years younger than my mother. My grandparents refused that request. Because they could not adopt my Aunt Josephine, I virtually became their adopted child. I often crawled up the stairs, even before I was able to confidently walk upstairs. I would often visit in the afternoon as my uncle returned from work. I was never turned away from having dinner upstairs. My parents often said that dinner was what attracted me to go upstairs, and they were not wrong. However, more than dinner attracted me.

Uncle Ignazio and Aunt Rosalia had dinner at 4:30 PM, earlier than my family – who ate around six o'clock. My grandparents had dinner even later, at 7 o'clock. As a child, on many evenings I made the rounds of the three homes, having three dinners. I did this as much as for attention as for food – I loved being the only child at dinner. The joke (or at least I thought it was a joke) was that one meal was not sufficient for me. I was a big eater. Looking back, I really enjoyed the attention I received, especially from my Uncle Ignazio and from Nonna: both of them favored me among all the children.

When I began kindergarten, I went home for a short period of time after school, then immediately went out to play or to visit my relatives. I was a responsible kid and my mother, who was always at home, was not concerned with my absence. She knew where I was – I was being cared for by relatives, and thus I was one less child she had to care for.

Being with my Aunt Rosalia was different from visiting at my grandmother's home, though both were home alone all day long. The main difference was that Rosalia spoke English. I had no difficulty understanding my aunt during the day, before my uncle returned home from work. Rosalia's home was neat and clean. There were no children there to mess things up. I was careful not to mess her home.

Aunt Rosalia also participated more directly in my upbringing than did my grandmother. Aunt Rosalia was not hesitant to offer her opinion to my mother, who was seven years younger, about my upbringing. On more than one occasion Rosalia cautioned my mother not to spank me too often. Rosalia did not believe in spanking (or as we would have said "hitting") a child. I appreciated her intervening when I was being disciplined by my mother.[20]

Aunt Rosalia paid attention to my grooming as well. I recall that she cautioned my mother about burning my ears with kerosene as a means to rid me of lice. Acquiring lice in the early 1940s was not unusual in our neighborhood. We called lice "bugs." When Aunt Rosalia saw that my ears were singed from a kerosene soaking, she took on the task of combing my

---

20 As I mentioned earlier, my father worked long hours, so he was often not home to discipline me. I cannot recall my father ever spanking me. He did yell at me, but he never spanked me.

hair with a fine-tooth comb to catch and kill the lice. This was a safe and much more pleasant way to rid me of lice than was kerosene.

I also ran errands for my Uncle Ignazio and Aunt Rosalia. I could go to the corner store without crossing a street and could pick up a needed item or two. One of the items I often bought was tobacco snuff, which came in a little blue package. There were no restrictions on selling tobacco to a seven-year-old. After I brought the snuff back to their home, it was transferred to little snuff container that had mother-of-pearl and a silver symbol inlaid on its lid. My uncle and aunt – and my grandmother – would take a "pinch" of tobacco between their thumb and forefinger and inhale it first through one nostril and then the other. They did not smoke, but they did use tobacco. My parents did not use snuff; my father smoked cigarettes, and my mother never inhaled anything. She occasionally puffed on a cigarette to be social.

Aunt Rosalia and Uncle Ignazio played a very important role for me in the life of our "village," but they were only two members of the large group that I called family. The doors to each of the three households at 412 Busti Avenue were always open to me. As a preschooler, although I slept at home, I spent my daytime indoor hours divided among the three homes. I did not have to go next door, or even as far as the front sidewalk – let alone across the street – to be with family. There were few restrictions on my visiting grandparents, uncles, aunts, and great uncles and aunts. All I had to say was "I'm going to Aunt Rosalia's" or "I'm going to Nonna's."

Grandma "Nonna" – Angela

As a 26-year-old in 1910, Angela had immigrated to the United States from Sicily to meet my grandfather, who had arrived three years earlier. I know very little about the three-year difference in their arrivals, and it remains unclear to me when and where my grandparents were married. When Angela arrived at Ellis Island, the ship's manifest (Italia) listed her as Angela Pilletteri, not as Angela Gardo, her married name. Marriage records from the Buffalo parish they attended were lost in a fire decades ago. If Angela and Benedetto were married in Sicily, Angela would have had an easier access to the United States as the wife of a resident alien. No one in my family ever questioned their marriage, the date, location and general circumstances, at least not publicly.

My Nonna, then Angela Piliterri (circa 1900-1905), standing. I estimate she was around 19 or 20 years old when this picture was taken.

Angela did not have much of a formal education. What education she received consisted of a few years at a Catholic convent in Sicily, so I was told. The formal Italian language was not yet fully adopted by Sicilian schools when she attended, especially in the village in which she had lived. While formal Italian may have been taught in some schools, Italian dialects were spoken throughout Italy, especially in Sicily. The Sicilian dialect is harsh, more so than other Italian dialects. Angela did not learn English after coming to the United States; my grandmother was able to communicate effectively only with family and Sicilian immigrants. Even at her death, after living in the United States for 44 years, Angela spoke almost no English. One English word she used was "pop," which is what we called soda. She enjoyed 7-UP, a citrus flavored soft drink that reminded her of Sicily.

Angela was never employed outside the house; in fact, she rarely left the house for any reason. She felt overwhelmed by the larger non-Italian community of Buffalo. I never saw her venture further than the street curb to meet a vegetable or fruit peddler's wagon. Angela was a recluse, which I did not fully grasp, while she was alive. She was so much a recluse that she did not attend Sunday Mass. She transformed her bedroom into a shrine, with statues, portraits of Jesus, Mary and Joseph, a crucifix, and candles.

In her late 60s, my grandmother contracted breast cancer. She had to leave the house, to be transported by car to a doctor and then later to a hospital for treatment. She died at home in 1954, when she was 69. Cancer was never discussed in my presence. I was surprised and shocked when I learned of her death. I was not aware that she was in an advanced stage of cancer. She died early on a Monday morning, but she had asked the night before why I was not at her home for Sunday dinner – as I was often reminded after her death. As a 16-year-old high school student I had other interests that competed with Sunday dinners at Grandma's.

Most in our family recognized that Grandma Angela was a recluse. I later learned that Angela suffered from depression and vertigo, and that she was an alcoholic. These diagnoses were not professional descriptions but guesses of illness made by family members. I am sure the term vertigo was not used by anyone in my family at the time, and not understood until much later. Someone who drank was called a "drunk," not an alcoholic; my grandmother was offered the courtesy of being described as "someone who likes her wine."

Family "secrets" and "old world" carryovers from a closed Sicilian society affected traditions and behavior and had continuing impact on members of my family. The impact on behavior based on secrets varied among the three generations – family members had differing views about what could or could not be discussed. I learned years later that my grandmother was two years older than my grandfather; this was clearly something that could not be discussed. Although Busti Avenue was separated from a Sicilian village by an ocean, life on Busti – embedded in Buffalo's West Side – definitely shared cultural roots with life in Sicily.

My grandmother had a sense of caring for me that I understood as a youngster. She knew that I was afraid of ghosts. I don't know how I became afraid of ghosts and monsters. Perhaps it was the horror movies I was able to attend without adult supervision. In 1944 – at age 6 – I saw *The Mummy's Curse* starring Lon Chaney and it scared the *bleep* out of me; I did not often get up from hiding under the seat during the entire movie.

I also suspect I developed a fear of ghosts and monsters because I slept on the window side of the bed at home. When I slept at my grandmother's house she would check on me before I went to sleep and remind me that I should only be afraid of live people – not ghosts. I could not share my fear of ghosts with my parents. After all, I was the oldest boy.

My grandmother always welcomed me as company. I knew there would always be someone home when I visited. She enjoyed my company. She was home alone each day when the men (her husband and brother and two sons) and the women were either at work or in school. I became an "only" child again at my grandmother's home in the "front".

Grandpa "Nonno"– Benedetto

My grandfather, Benedetto Gardo, was the head of the household. He spoke "broken" English, which was a valuable asset for an immigrant in the early 1900's. My grandfather pronounced Buffalo as *Boof-alow*. Benedetto never lost his Sicilian roots. He would always be cautious and wary of meeting anyone for the first time, especially a governmental official. At work at the New York Central Railroad Freight House, Benedetto could speak English well enough to interpret management's work instructions to the Sicilian labor crew he supervised. His ability to speak English and translate work orders into a Sicilian dialect was of great value on the job. Benedetto could also complete work status reports for management, and he could supervise the completion of work assignments. He was a "Boss" at the freight house – and he prospered. He was much respected on the job, at home, and in the community.

Gertrude reported my grandfather's 1939 annual salary at the Freight House as $1700, when the median national income was $956. My grandfather's income was almost twice as much as that of the laborers in his crew at the time. The salary he received was also among the highest reported in the census enumeration district. His salary was about that of a skilled craftsman, such as a tool and die maker. In addition, because my grandfather owned the 412 Busti Avenue property, he also received three monthly rents totaling $65. His total annual income was thus approximately $2500. That was "big" money, especially for a Buffalo Sicilian laborer. Although Benedetto had no formal skill or craft, he had leadership qualities.

As a young man, Benedetto was strikingly handsome and imposing. Many thought he resembled the movie star Errol Flynn. Most Italians who knew Benedetto, referred to him as a "six footer." Benedetto was quite tall for a Sicilian, but he mostly likely was 5 foot 10 or 11 inches tall, not six feet. Any Italian man within an inch or two of being 6 feet tall was a "six footer." (In the 1940's, Frank Sinatra was reputed to be five feet eleven by most Italians, not the five feet eight inches that he most likely was.) Nonno carried himself taller than a tape measure would document. Most Italian men, especially Sicilians, looked up to him, both figuratively and literally. To be a tall man was valued among Italians (and non-Italians as well).

The Gardo Children: Intra-Generational Acculturation and Assimilation

Catholic families in the early 20th century were usually large by contemporary standards; a family having five, six, seven or more children was not unusual. Large families, especially Catholic families, were just large families – common at that time. What I found less obvious until I started thinking about this was the impact of the passing of time between the oldest and youngest children in a family. This was definitely true in the Gardo household.

The two oldest Gardo children, my mother, Grace, and my Aunt Phyllis, were born a year apart, in 1911 and 1912 – shortly after my grandmother's arrival in America. Even as Americans, the two oldest girls were exposed to a stronger Sicilian culture than were the three younger girls. In contrast, there were expanding economic and social opportunities for the three youngest girls during the war years – opportunities that were not available when the two older girls were the same age. The nearly two decades that passed between the births of the oldest and youngest children saw the development of different cultural norms and mores and had a wide range of impacts on the seven children, and especially on the five girls. The effects of Americanization and assimilation were evident in the Gardo family over the 17-year period which separated their births. Seventeen years represents a significant time spread which I interpret as "generational" in its impact.[21]

Change was more pronounced for the Gardo girls in general than it was for the Gardo boys, Buddy (Bartholomew) and Russell (Rosario). The boys had few parental restrictions, as long as they did not get into trouble with the police. All the girls had restrictions upon them, though the older ones were even more restricted than the younger ones.

My mother Grace, the oldest child, was not far removed from being born in Sicily. She married an Italian immigrant— my father. Neither of the two oldest girls completed grade school. They entered the workforce in their early teens. The two oldest girls may as well have been born in Sicily,

---

21 There is a great deal of scholarly disagreement regarding the length of a "generation." The Greatest Generation is often categorized as being born between 1901 and 1927; the Baby Boom generation is recognized as being born between 1946 and 1964; Millenials are classified as being born between 1981 and 1996. What is clear is that the social forces acting on the oldest and the youngest Gardo children – and especially on the girls – had changed rather substantially for those born in 1911 and 1928.

given my family's, especially my grandmother's, shallow American roots at the time.

The younger girls were less likely to accept some of the restrictions placed on them than were their two older sisters; they received more education and were more independent. Rose, the third daughter who responded to the census questions, completed two years of high school. She then left school to enter the workforce. The two youngest Gardo girls, Mary and Josephine, both attended high school and by all family accounts were excellent students. Mary was awarded the Buffalo School system's Jesse Ketchum Medal for academic excellence at PS1 Grammar School. She excelled in art and completed a two-year commercial art program at Buffalo Girl's High School. Josephine (referred to as Josie), who was 12 years old in 1940 (reported inaccurately as 11 years old in the Census), graduated from Grover Cleveland High School in 1946. She was the first family member to graduate from high school. Josie was not celebrated as having graduated and certainly not encouraged to continue her education beyond high school.[22]

The three youngest girls – Rose, Mary and Josephine – reached maturity during "the War years" (1941-45). They had fewer restrictions than the older girls had in regard to marriage. Going out with men was still monitored by my grandparents but was much less restricted for the two youngest girls, Mary and Josephine. The younger women adopted the more liberated American lifestyle. The three youngest Gardo women married non-Italians, and two of them were not at, first, married in the Catholic Church.

All the female Gardos wanted to fit into America *as "Americans."* They were enmeshed in a process of assimilation and acculturation, adapting to American culture and norms, although to different extents and at different rates. Americanization was not always quickly and fully achieved,

---

22 Unfortunately for Josephine, my twin sisters, Kathy and Angie, were born the same month that Josephine graduated from high school. The twins' birth received all the attention and Josephine's graduation was little celebrated and passed mostly unrecognized.

even among the younger Gardo sisters. Assimilation came with some tension, uncertainty and sometimes with conflict seeking sought-after parental approval. There were cross pressures on parents and children. The three youngest Gardo women were presented opportunities such as jobs and boyfriends – and at times, these were shielded from parental view. New liberating lifestyles were adopted, which in retrospect appear relatively mild – but any change entailed walking the line between the old ways and the new.

I vividly recall an incident involving my youngest aunt, Josephine, wanting to go to a movie theater when she was 18 years old. She needed me to accompany her to the Niagara movie theater, a mere block and a half away from home. She came to our house in the "back" to ask my mother if I could go with her. My mother said of course, but then said that I needed to finish my dinner. I was pulled away from the table, but not from dinner. I became an eight-year-old chaperone – taking my unfinished plate of pasta and peas with me to finish while watching a movie on the big screen. I don't remember the movie, but I do remember that pasta. I did not have any popcorn, but I finished my pasta at the theater.

The Gardo Boys: Role Models?

The boys were not subject to the same restrictions as the girls. Bartholomew "Buddy" (born in 1915) and Rosario "Russell" (born in 1917) were my mother's brothers and were employed as laborers in 1940. Neither had finished high school. My grandfather had expected that Buddy, the oldest son and his "favorite," would continue his education – but Buddy did not attend college after returning from the U.S. Army during World War II. There was not any expectation that Russell, let alone that any of the girls, would attend college.

Buddy "volunteered" to join the United States Army in 1941, before Pearl Harbor and the United States' entry into World War II – but this was something of a family joke, as he did not willingly volunteer. Buddy was subjected to an "early" draft notice from the Selective Service Board, and he "enlisted" in the US Army in September 1941. The family story that circulated to explain Buddy's "early draft notice" was that he got into a minor legal incident, probably a barroom "scrape" (never referred to as a brawl). Buddy was offered a "choice": submit to an early enlistment in the United States Army or serve a jail sentence. No surprise – his choice was the early draft.

Because he had "joined" the U.S. Army prior to the United States' declaration of war, he was considered by many to be part of the regular standing Continental Army. He was awarded a yellow service ribbon, The American Defense Service Medal (ADSM). This award signified that a serviceman (or woman) was in the armed forces between September 8, 1939 and December 7, 1941. This was a period recognized by President Roosevelt's Proclamation of a Limited National Emergency (Proclamation 2352) prior to the United States' declaration of war. The ADSM was discontinued the day after Congress declared War on Japan on December 8, 1941.

The "yellow ribbon" had *real* value for Buddy. Before WWII the U.S. Army was quite small in size; it consisted mostly of career Army regulars, and few draftees. The award was for "Regular Military Personnel" who served in the Armed forces in the unsettling and dangerous two-year period before Pearl Harbor. The ADSM award recognized an inductee's commitment to defense of the nation, and not just a response to being drafted into the armed services.

While at a saloon near the military base during his basic training, Buddy was part of yet another barroom brawl (scrape) involving several dozen enlisted men. The military police (MP) broke up the fight and commenced to take those involved to the "stockade" (jail). A WWI veteran Master Sergeant spotted the ADSM Ribbon that Buddy wore and intervened on his behalf. Buddy did not have to go to the stockade as did the other solders engaged in the incident. Buddy, who had been forced to "volunteer," had obtained a status among the regular non-commissioned officers (Non-Coms) as an "old timer." I still chuckle when I think of what those Non-Coms might have said if they had only known how Buddy had "volunteered."

Buddy also had quite a fortunate experience for the duration of his military service in the US Army: he was assigned as a mess hall cook to a medical unit in Maryland that conducted physical examinations for inductees entering the service. Buddy was an outstanding Italian chef. He had learned to cook by watching and assisting his father and mother preparing meals. Buddy had accompanied his father on weekly shopping trips to buy ingredients for meals, such as olive oil, salami, provolone cheese, macaroni and other Italian staples that were not familiar to non-Italians at that time. Buddy had taken over much of the cooking responsibilities at home as his mother withdrew from active participation in running the household. He had become a damn good Italian cook; he was really a creative artist in the kitchen.

Although not an official chef, he was considered a chef and treated like one by the unit commander. Buddy was soon promoted to Mess Sergeant of a medical unit. He was in charge of the entire Mess Hall – all operations and personnel, including purchasing ingredients for meals. He was stationed north of Baltimore and visited the city's Italian neighborhoods to purchase imported foods from Italy.

His favored status as an "Italian Gourmet Mess Sergeant" had important consequences for Buddy. The medical unit commander, who was quite taken with Buddy's creative cooking skills, designated him as "necessary personnel." Buddy was given continuous exemptions from assignments that might have taken him to activities in Europe, possibly including exposure to combat. Buddy never left the States to serve in theaters of combat. He served most of his four-year enlistment in Aberdeen, Maryland, close enough to visit family in Buffalo several times a year.

Just as important to Buddy as his military assignment was being stationed near Pimlico Racetrack in Baltimore, which he frequented on free weekends and holidays during the racing season. He continued to be a thoroughbred racing fan and pari-mutuel bettor for the remainder of his life. He did not seek to professionally pursue his culinary talents and skills when he was discharged in 1945 – even though having been honorably discharged he had access to the GI Bill of Rights to pay for attending a culinary program. After the war he became a beer salesman – at which he was very good.

Buddy remained a bachelor his entire life. He had several long-term female companions with whom he lived. He hung around the neighborhood, socializing with his many longtime friends. He was well known on the West Side of Buffalo.

Buddy congratulated me late in his life – recognizing our role reversals. He congratulated me for "making something" of myself. He said that he was proud that I became a professor. I gave him a copy of my Ph. D. dissertation. I am not sure he read it, and if he did, I am not sure he would have understood it. He felt he had not taken advantage of his military service benefits to further his education. I thought about how I was a professor, while Buddy had a lot of fun in how he approached and lived life. We each saw value in the path the other took, though not consciously realizing that there had been changes in expectations and opportunities in the generation that separated us.

The second Gardo son, Russell, was classified as 4F – not physically fit for military service – at the beginning of WWII. He had lost an eye as an eleven-year-old while playing with a knife. Like many of the events of that era, there are several versions of how Russell lost his eye.

The family story I believe is most accurate indicated that Russell and some other boys were throwing a knife at a telephone pole to see which of them could make it stick closest to a target. The knife ricocheted off the pole and hit Russell in the eye. The eye was penetrated, yet still attached to its socket. My grandmother did not act immediately to seek medical care. She thought the eye would heal and gave Russell home care for two days before having a doctor examine the extent of damage to his eye. I remain uncertain about whether a speedy visit to a doctor would have saved Russell's eye from the knife wound.

Russell became a family man. He married and had two daughters, Angela and Josephine. He was generous. He always offered my family assistance, especially when we needed transportation. He owned a pickup truck which was used to collect junk – especially items of value that could be sold, such as copper wire. On one occasion he came to our house with several pounds of copper wire in rubber casing. He put the wire in a large metal trash can. He started a fire, creating thick billowing black smoke covering a large portion of the neighborhood. Police never arrived to investigate. Russell picked up the bare copper and took it to a junk dealer to be sold.

The Neighborhood

While most of my family's time was spent at our compound on Busti Ave., our village extended out to some of the neighborhood businesses. Those places where we purchased food and drink were particularly important.

A chicken market was located at the end of our block; it provided freshly killed and dressed poultry. My aunt and mother bought mostly young chickens for roasting, or older, tough chickens for soup and tomato sauces. They sometimes bought capons to roast for Sunday dinners or for special occasions or holidays such as Thanksgiving and Christmas.

Capons were an Italian tradition and delicacy; they are neutered roosters, specially fattened for eating, which makes them very tender and plump. Capons were generally 9 to 10 pounds – sizeable, but not the size of present-day turkeys. Thanksgiving often meant capons – along with turkeys – especially at my grandparents' home. Our Thanksgiving dinner always started with antipasta, then a pasta, vegetables then capon and sausage, and finally concluded with a salad and a mixture of roasted nuts. My grandfather said that only in restaurants do they start dinner with salad. He said Italians eat salad after dinner to clean their palette, although he did not use that word. I guess Thanksgiving at our home was "Italianized" – but nevertheless we were all thankful.

I would often accompany Aunt Rosalia and my mother to the poultry market, where clerks would pick up the bird we selected. The bird's neck was slit and then the bird was tipped over with its head down so that the blood would flow into a funnel leading to a barrel below. After this was completed, the dead bird was dipped in hot water to loosen the feathers. After a sufficient time of soaking the bird to soften many feathers, the bird was then put on a rotary machine with rubber spikes on a spindle that spun very fast to knocked off the feathers. After being on the machine, the bird was relatively clean, but still had a number of feather roots which would be pulled out at home, one at a time. The killing and dressing of a bird to our specifications took no longer than 15 minutes – so we waited. We also waited to be sure that the bird we ordered was the one we took home.

Chicken in the 1940s was a specialty food and not an inexpensive food for daily meals, as it is today. It seems that those chickens tasted a lot better than the chickens of today. For certain, the chickens were fresh – after all, we were buying them at a "slaughterhouse."

My Uncle Ignazio would stop at Frank's Tavern on the corner of our block for a couple of beers on his way home from work. I called Frank's a "bar," not a tavern. I knew my uncle's schedule and sometimes met him at Frank's, where he would buy me birch beer. Birch beer is similar to root beer, but a bit more-tart. It had a kick which tickled my nose. I felt like I was part of the "work gang" at the bar at Frank's. As a 6-year-old, I was throwing birch beers down as if they were glasses of real beer with my uncle and the other workers.

Frank's Tavern also had a kitchen that served food. The restaurant section of Frank's had a half dozen tables in the backroom for dining. It was the first and the only restaurant I remember visiting with my family and relatives. One of the coolest parts of the restaurant were doorbells on the wall at each table that would be rung to alert the waiter that he was needed. The waiter was always a man. There was only one waiter for the entire restaurant portion of the bar – but he always responded to the bell quickly, never leaving us searching for service.

The "bar" food served was traditional southern Italian, particularly Sicilian dishes. Of course, there was spaghetti and meatballs, Italian sausage, and lasagna. Two dishes that were local specialties – and my favorites – were fava beans and tripe. During the summer there were also dishes of clams and crabs, most likely shipped up to Buffalo from the Chesapeake Bay. Clams and crabs were often eaten outside at an outdoor clam stand appended to Frank's.

I do not recall pizza being served at Frank's in the 1940's; at that time pizza was a plain dish, served at home as a snack or as a quick meal. Pizza was never eaten as the main meal. At home pizzas were decorated simply with tomato sauce and anchovies (which are common on Sicilian pizzas) and topped with parmesan – not mozzarella – cheese.

* * * * *

My family, our compound, our neighborhood – my village – provided a safe and comfortable environment for me. Life was secure and welcoming. I belonged in all three households. I was part of a large family that wanted me to respect and appreciate all of them. I was an extension of the lives of my parents, and of the previous generation who had emigrated to the United States. I was part of a family with roots and pride, which I understood without having to be told. Living at 412 Busti Avenue was the lens through which I viewed, experienced, and interpreted life as a young child. This would continue until my immediate family moved in 1946 – and the village was no longer my daily reality.

We were an extended immigrant family spanning three generations, negotiating American culture as best we could. Gertrude had visited the front house before she came to see my parents, and all but one family member was revealed to her. Their individual stories would elude Gertrude; she was there to count, not to learn about the nuances of our lives. And there was a part of life Gertrude – and the 1940 census – could not even begin to capture: my life outdoors.

CHAPTER 4:

THE JOYOUS OUTDOORS

Being home was pleasant, secure and comfortable. But our home was small; there was little space to play without getting in the way of my parents, or having my younger brothers get in my way. The kitchen was the primary play area and the busiest room in my house most of the day. There were few toys at home. No radio. No "real" books, only romance magazines such as True Confessions. Television did not exist when we lived on Busti Avenue; TV would not come to our home until 1951, five years after we moved to Grant Street. And I have few memories of starting school, or of any school activities from my early days, except that I was not very good at coloring objects between the lines.

Outdoor play is what I remember most vividly. Much of what gave me joy and what I remember as good times happened when I was outdoors. I would suggest that many of my most important educational experiences took place outside – on front sidewalks and in backyards. (I did not "play in the streets;" that was just a figure of speech that adults used.) Playing and exploring and just hanging out with neighborhood kids was real fun. What I will describe about play on Busti Avenue all occurred before I was eight and a half, although my memory of those years blurs together.

Outside play provided me an escape from family restrictions, and especially from my mother. My father was usually at work or sleeping during the day in preparation for his night shift. Of course, being outdoors among playmates, did not mean I had *complete* freedom. As we played, we were often observed by stay-at-home-mothers and other neighborhood women. In my case, my grandmother was often on the porch (weather permitting), keeping an eye on me.

The Neighborhood

My home was just a few blocks from the Erie Canal and Lake Erie: this defined the West Side of Buffalo. This was the turf of Sicilians and was considered a dangerous place by many nonresidents, Italians and non-Italians alike. I did not have any concept of the "West Side" as the den of *mafioso*. I never witnessed a violent act near my home. As far as I was concerned, the West Side was safe and secure and where I belonged.

Only after we moved to a different neighborhood outside the Sicilian West Side did I come to understand that I had lived in an area that was viewed with apprehension by many people. The West Side had a reputation as a place where hoodlums hung out and organized crime flourished. I later found out that this was somewhat deserved, but it wasn't this way for West Side children. As long as people minded their own business, the streets were safe – especially for children.

Being outdoors also provided an important set of personal relationships that I had to accommodate differently than I did with adults who spoke a "foreign" language at several levels, as they were trying to adapt to a new country. Most of the kids I played with were first- or second-generation Americans. We sought a sense of liberation from our more rigid and "different" home lives. Joe Di Geralimo, who lived three doors from me, was the only Italian kid whose parents were "modern" – they did not speak Italian at home or have an Italian accent. As playmates we learned from and influenced one another – creating a new world in our young generation. Home and the streets, encompassing all of two or three city blocks, had contrasting effects on my language, behavior, and values.

Being outdoors in my neighborhood gave me a great deal of freedom and let me escape into games and make connections about the world around me. For example, I associated a popular 1942 song, "The Jersey Bounce," with Jersey Street, which was a block from my home. Jersey Street had a hill which I thought was the "bounce" in the song. I thought it was neat to have a song named after a nearby street.

My outdoor play with other kids was liberating. Beyond a certain age, there was no strict supervision of our play or of outdoor activity of any kind by parents. My home life in all three households was very good, but not carefree. I had to behave all the time. When I was outdoors, I acted and talked in a way that provided personal expression that other boys under 10 years old understood – we were all in the same boat.

My play activities were exclusively among boys who were about my age (some were a couple years older, or a year or so younger) on the front sidewalks or in backyards, vacant lots, and at the corner hangout. We all attended the same public school and there was not more than a grade level of difference among us.[23] My neighborhood did not have designated play areas, such as playgrounds or tot lots. Public School No. 1, which I attended, did not have a playground.

In the first half of the 1940's, World War II was a backdrop to most of my daily activities.[24] War was created daily, especially in outdoor play

23 Some boys who were older were in my grade level, having been held back a grade. It was not uncommon to be held back a year, in some cases two years, while in grammar school. The term we used at that time was someone didn't "pass a grade." I was unaware of any stigma, shame or a sense of failure attached to not being promoted to the next grade. Mostly boys failed a grade in school; I don't recall any girls failing. In 1946, when my family moved to our new home on Grant Street, a non-Italian working-class neighborhood, failing a grade or two was also not uncommon there.

24 The war was experienced a bit differently in my home than in most other families at that time. As the United States entered the war, many in the Gardo household, including my father, were Italians – not yet American citizens. This was important because of Italy's alliance with Germany. With my father being an Italian citizen, the FBI visited my home to see if there was a concealed two-way radio. There was no two-way radio. Yet, the incident became part of family folklore. I considered myself and my family to be Americans: we wanted victory against Germany, Japan and Italy. My father, aunts and uncles all participated in the war effort, either in the US armed forces or employed in the defense industry.

activities. As young kids, we would play war games, and we also played "cowboys and Indians." An important and memorable marker of my age was that I had just turned seven when World War II ended in 1945 – just a little more than a week after my birthday on August 25. The war's end came soon after two atomic bombs were dropped on Hiroshima and Nagasaki, Japan. I heard some older boys talk about the atomic bomb causing a chain-reaction. No one knew what that was, but we questioned whether the chain-reaction would stop before it reached us.

So, we shouted about cowboys killing Indians with a "bang-bang, you're dead, I got you;" or we played war against Nazis and Japs who we thought were evil. At that time, we described the enemies as Indians and Japs, not Native Americans and Japanese. Sensitivity in discussing minorities was several decades off into the future for me, and for the U.S. in general. Little did I know that we were discussing things that only young boys – less than 10 years old – would talk about. But our discussions belonged to us and gave us a sense of having our own world.

I remember outside play as generally safe from autos and other types of outdoor injuries. Busti Avenue was a one-way street, which adults considered to be safer than a two-way street as we only had to look in one direction for approaching traffic. But there were some exceptions.

My brother Benny was hit (more likely bumped or knocked down) by a car while he was playing in the street near our house. I guess I was supposed to keep an eye on him. I did not know he had gotten bumped by a car until my mother discovered him on her return from shopping. He wasn't seriously injured but being knocked down by that car frightened him. My mother started screaming when she saw him lying in the street. She brought him home, examined him and became even more upset. I was not sure what role, if any, I had played in him getting bumped by a car. My mother seemed more upset with herself and concerned about what the neighbors may have thought about her leaving me in charge of my little brother.

I once jumped and hung onto a passing pickup truck in front of our house. As I hung on to the truck, a sharp object – possibly a nail – dug into my elbow. That object created an open wound and left a scar that remains visible to this day. I remember thinking that my wound must have resembled Jesus' wounds upon the Cross.

Playing outside meant being with the kids on my block.[25] Houses on Busti were built close together, with little more than a five- or six-foot walkway between them. With houses so close together, a city block (a distance of no more than a couple of hundred yards) had many homes on each side of the street. Many houses also had two flats – one downstairs and one upstairs – and a few homes also had a cottage in back of the main house.[26]

Many neighborhood homes meant many children, with many on my city block about my age. Playmates were in abundance; there was no real need to venture to the next block seeking companions and playmates. Sidewalks, vacant lots and corner commercial establishments provided the spaces to play. As I look back I had no sense of being crowded or lacking space or needing a playground.

Buffalo was a collection of neighborhoods, many of which where ethnic in character. Even among Italians there were separate neighborhoods depending on the region of Italy from which the resident emigrated. There was reputed to be a powerful mafia boss in each neighborhood, as this was viewed by many Italians as beneficial for protecting the neighborhood from "real" criminals. Petty crime did not affect residents, who paid little attention to activities involving the most prominent criminal activity – gambling (crap games and playing the numbers).

---

25 As the oldest child in my family, I had no one my age to play with at home. I was close in age to my brother Benny, but four years older than Joey and six years older than Eugene. For me playing with them outdoors was out of the question. Outdoors they were my responsibility to watch over, rather than my playmates. I considered them to be burdens who interfered with my outdoor life.

26 With houses only a few a few feet from one another, next door often meant the "next to" door. There were only driveways separating houses in a couple of cases. Most houses had tiny backyards of no more than 20 x 10 feet. There were no side yards between homes. Next door neighbors did not have much privacy from one another. Even the small suburban bungalow tract homes built after WWII had much more space between homes than did our Busti neighborhood.

As I grew older, there were occasions when I ventured off my block and toward Lake Erie, less than a mile away. Around the block, by crossing Trenton Avenue, I could enter the Lakeview Public Housing Development, which we called the "Projects." In 1940, Lakeview Public Housing was among the first in the nation to be built by President Franklin Delano Roosevelt's Administration as part of the New Deal.[27] In the 1940s, the Projects housed exclusively white families; African-Americans were segregated into the Willert Park housing project about three miles away.[28] African Americans did not begin to live in the Lakeview Projects until the 1950s.

Lakeview Housing, circa mid-1940s. Photo: Buffalo Historical Society.

Lakeview Housing units were constructed of brick, with many walkways and much green grass surrounding the buildings. There was the magnificent Front Park a block away, bordering Lake Erie. Individual Lakeview Housing units were quite small, having either one or two bedrooms. There

---

27 Some brief information about the history of public housing in Buffalo can be found at https://buffaloah.com/surveys/PresReady/m.html.
28 Willert Park has been mostly abandoned since the early 2010s, but there is interest in reviving what was once the center of Buffalo's African-American community; see https://www.buffalorising.com/2019/05/willert-park-courts-announced-as-one-of-the-11-most-endangered-historic-places-in-the-united-states/.

were two types of building structures: one was a three-story walk-up with individual units opening into a hallway; the second type was a two-story structure with each unit having a single outdoor entrance. The two-story structures were placed in a row, similar to two-story motel units.

Lakeview Housing was occupied by working-class white families not much different than the people on my street. I had two relatives who lived in the Projects. My Aunt Mary's and my Uncle Russell's families both lived in the Projects. Aunt Mary lived in a third-floor walkup apartment. Uncle Russell lived in a two-story unit with an outside ground-level entrance. When I visited them I had no thought that they were poor. The Projects were only a different kind of housing as far as I was concerned. All the kids in my neighborhood – including those living in the Projects – attended the same public schools as all other neighborhood children.

I was unaware of any social stigma attached to public housing by adults, and there certainly was none for us kids. During World War II all housing was in short supply. Public housing was needed and was not considered to be just homes for the poor or needy. Indeed, the projects offered amenities that were not available on my street. Public housing provided the closest "open" space away from streets for children to play safely.

The Projects had tot lots with slides, swings, teeter totters, sand boxes, and my favorite – the monkey bars. The monkey bars were aluminum bars formed into three-foot squares stacked four wide and three high, extending up to nine feet high. There were no safety rails to prevent climbers from falling and getting injured. I suppose the monkey bars were included to take the place of trees to climb.

Exploring with Friends

At home, adults chose conversations and guided communication. Obviously, there was nothing unusual about this; what was unusual was the nature of my surroundings and associations that I began to recognize as I reviewed the data from the 1940 US Census. Being outdoors was an unsupervised community that was an extension of – but very different than – the community of my extended family.

I didn't engage in conversations with adults about my outdoor activities and behavior. I was asked few questions and shared little about what I did "outside." If I had questions about something I heard on the street that interested me, I didn't ask my parents. I posed questions to playmates who often did not know any more than I did. Some of the answers offered to my questions were truly inventive.

For example, during the 1940s few neighborhood residents used funeral parlors or mortuaries to provide services for the deceased. Wakes and viewings were held in homes. A wreath was placed at the front door of a home to alert all passersby that someone had died. The casket with the body was usually placed in the living room for viewing, surrounded by flowers, wreaths and extra folding chairs for mourners. After the wake was held in the home, usually for a period of three days, there was a funeral procession to the church. Virtually all individuals I was aware of who had passed away were Catholic and then the deceased was taken to a cemetery. Not just any cemetery, but a Catholic cemetery, where burial was not permitted for non-Catholics. And at the time I thought heaven was closed to non-Catholics as well.[29]

As a seven-year-old I visited several wakes of individuals I did not know. Visiting a wake was not quite a game, but an activity of curiosity. One wake I visited with a couple of friends was that of an "old" man (who was probably younger than I currently am). We looked at the corpse in the coffin and made comments about old people, as if death would never occur for us. There were a lot of flowers in the room.

I went to another wake with a group of buddies. We visited the viewing of a seven-year-old boy who had lived down the street from me. I did not know him when he was alive; I don't think I had ever even seen him. The boy died of cancer. Viewing someone who had died at such a young

---

29 There was no thought or awareness of cremation. I did not know there was such a thing as cremation, let alone that a body could be burned.

age was of concern to me. I was puzzled that death could come to someone so young, without getting hit by a car or drowning.[30]

One of my buddies who attended the viewing of the seven-year-old with me made an off-hand comment that the boy looked a lot bigger dead than he did when alive. My buddy said that maybe bodies grow even after a person dies. For quite a while, I thought a child continued to grow after death. Upon reflection, the reality was that the boy had been being treated in the hospital for quite a while and grew taller out of my buddy's sight.

I never mentioned that I had visited wakes to any adults, especially my parents – who never asked. The consequences of viewing wakes stayed with me a long time. People – especially young people – died, and then what happened? If their body remained to be viewed, what went to heaven or to hell? Going to wakes was not quite entertainment, but something of interest to do. This was an example of our unsupervised activities.

On a few occasions, as an 8-year-old, play took me off the block to the open spaces along the nearby railroad tracks by Lake Erie. There weren't any fences or barriers between my home and the railroad tracks or Lake Erie; there were open fields of grass, weeds and prickly thistles and milk pod plants. There were also "Victory Gardens" on public and railroad land; they were tended during the day by older, retired persons. Victory Gardens were our community's contribution to the war effort, along with neighborhood paper and scrap drives.

No one was ever struck by a train even though we played on the tracks. We pretended we were the "Indians" we saw at the movies. We put our ears to the track to listen for trains. We also put pennies on the tracks so that a passing train would flatten them.

Joe Di Geralimo, the playmate I mentioned before who lived a few doors down from me, was able to get bullets for a handgun from his father's cabinet. Joe, two other boys, and I built a bonfire in the open fields near the

---

30 A first-grade classmate of mine had drowned in Lake Erie during the summer between first and second grade. When I saw his photo in the newspaper I was not sure how a photo had been taken if he was dead. I did not attend his wake.

railroad tracks. Joe threw the bullets into the fire. The four of us hid behind some logs and rocks to wait for the bullets to explode. We didn't have a clue as to how long it would take for the bullets to explode to turn the fire into "gunfire." I didn't know exactly how many bullets Joe threw into the fire— it was just "a handful." We immediately ducked as we threw the bullets into the fire. We were not sure when all the bullets had exploded. We were fortunate that we waited a sufficient time after the last bullets had exploded. No one was "shot" – but we had been exposed to gunfire without a gun. Dangerous? Yes.

We never spoke of this to anyone else. We were just a band of second- and- third graders having fun. How would we have explained to our parents – let alone the authorities – if someone had suffered a bullet wound without a gun?

On another occasion my buddies and I built a fire to light some rolled up newspapers that we had brought to the open fields. We rolled the newspapers up in tight cylinders to resemble cigarettes (or more likely cigars) and smoked them. We inhaled the burning paper, at least once, thinking that we were smoking as adults did.

Catalpa trees were prominent in the area. They produced seed pods that we called "Indian Cigars." We tried to smoke them as well. The cigars did not taste good when we smoked them – but they did taste a bit better than the newspapers. My inclination to smoke was put on hold for a long time after these experiments.

The open fields were also used by construction companies to store building materials; these included a huge sand pile; it may have been about two stories high. The sand was to be mixed with cement to make concrete for construction. The large mountain of sand was located in an open, unfenced field that was not supervised during the evenings or on weekends.

My brother Benny and a couple of his friends began digging a tunnel in the sand "mountain" to create a hiding place. The sand pile was near the waterfront open space and railroad tracks, away from adult observation. I could not stop Benny from tunneling. I was afraid for him, as well as concerned because I did not go into the tunnel after him. The sand mound was unstable and dangerous. It would not have taken much for the sand to cave in upon anyone who was in the tunnel. I was frightened to dig and enter the sand pile myself, so I ran home the two blocks to tell my father. He came and pulled my brother out of the tunnel before anything happened. My father was angry at both of us. He was angry at Benny for being inside a hand-dug tunnel and mad at me for not stopping him. My father was not a very good lecturer, but he let us have a verbal tongue lashing that time. As usual, we didn't receive a spanking from him. Spanking us was my mother's job. Benny and I never returned to the sand mound.[31]

There was a bakery at the end of my block, kitty corner across the intersection. The bakery specialized in making donuts of many types, especially my favorites, cream filled and glazed donuts. The smell of baking donuts filled the entire neighborhood. The inviting fragrance was impossible to ignore. That smell of donuts was so good it was almost like eating the donuts themselves. But the captivating aroma of freshly baked donuts was not enough for young boys. We had to eat them.

The bakers cooled the donuts on racks by open windows – first floor windows, no less – during warmer weather. The donuts were within easy reaching distance from outside if we stood on a crate, box or upside-down trash can to reach through the window. There were many of these items nearby to stand on. We had no problem reaching our prize – free warm donuts. We placed the donuts in boxes, paper bags or kept individual donuts in our hands while we ran around the block to secure a hiding place

31 That was hardly Benny's last adventure. A few years after our sand pile experience, Benny's adventurousness and my restraint again came to the fore. In the open space a few blocks from our home (behind Buffalo State College) was a 100-foot tall mushroom-shaped water pressure tower. Benny and a friend of ours climbed the ladder of the water tower, arriving at a circular platform around its top. There were no guardrails on the ladder to protect climbers from falling. Benny and his friend reached the top of the tower platform; I remained on the ground watching them ascend. This time I did not run home to alert my father. Benny was on his own and would remain so from then on through his life. The view from the tower must've been magnificent!

Benny passed on as I was preparing to send this manuscript out to publishers in January 2021.

to eat them. Cooling donuts were easy targets of opportunity for unsupervised kids on the street. We were engaging in petty larceny – or put plainly, stealing donuts – to have a most delicious treat. I can still remember how good they tasted. And we didn't have to pay for them.

There was a grocery store at each end of my block; I could walk to two grocery stores without crossing a street. We did most food shopping at these corner grocers. There was also an A&P supermarket two blocks away on Niagara Street, which was a main throughfare of the West Side. Italian import stores, restaurants, bakeries, and a movie theater were all located on Niagara Street as well.

Food shopping was very different than it is now. Many goods had to be packaged or wrapped by the clerk (there were few prepackaged food products at that time). Many items had to be individually wrapped, such as macaroni products. Macaroni came in wooden 50- pound boxes. Each purchase of macaroni was weighed and individually wrapped in white paper kept on a large roll and tied with string from a large spool. No one – not my family, not our neighbors – bought macaroni that came in a cardboard one-pound box. Long macaroni such as spaghetti and linguine were always wrapped in white paper. Short macaroni such as penne and shells were weighed and put into a paper bag.

Canned goods were often kept on high shelves. The items had to be reached by the clerk with a 5-foot grasping pole with crab-like pinchers on the end. Cans from the top shelves were grasped and brought down, one at a time. There was some effort by the clerk in reaching the items, lowering them down, and walking them back to the counter to be placed with all the other items that had been ordered.

One activity that I participated in at the corner grocer with other kids my age still makes me chuckle. Two or three boys (including me) would go into the grocery store and order a number of items. As all the items were being brought down, we would run out of the store laughing. The game was to order groceries and run out before the clerk noticed. We put the clerk through so much work! This game was great fun. The clerks were often the store owners. They never followed up on my "misdeeds" by telling my parents – or at least my parent did not ask me about my shopping experiences.

Morality with Friends

I did not attend Catholic schools, nor did I get much guidance from church officials (priests and nuns). I received little formal religious education at home. I did receive much guidance and instruction on good behavior. I would say – from my perspective now – that I received solid moral grounding. I had a very strong family who expected me to be a "good boy." My parents worked very hard and brought their six children up to do the right thing. They provided us with excellent values but little formal religious instruction.

My mother in particular was extremely generous. She was a giving person and spiritual in her own way. She did not attend church often when I was young. On one occasion, she questioned whether baby Jesus was the same person as the adult Jesus depicted in pictures, paintings, and statues. It did not occur to me until much later that my mother probably meant where did all the years go from when Jesus was a baby to Jesus being 30 years old and was considered the Son of God. I thought her comment was silly at the time; after all, my mother had asked me when I entered grade school whether California was part of the United States. She was quite intelligent and clever but unaware of many things that she had not been taught or did not experience. She saw things that puzzled her, but she was not knowledgeable or very articulate about religion and many other topics such as history or geography.

My father did not engage in conversations about religion. He was honest and a very decent person – the kind of person that people would say was a good man or the "salt of the earth."

I have no memory of attending church services with my parents. I know we were all together when I was baptized. My mother did tell me that once I yelled out that my father had gotten a new suit at a Sunday Mass when I was three years old. I went to church each Sunday with neighborhood kids. We attended mass in a church chapel separate from adults.

Much of what I learned as a youngster, including religion and morality, took place outside. Three episodes that touch on morality, if not exactly religion, come to mind.

I remember being sent to a grocery store, and the clerk made an error in giving me change for the purchase I had made – I had given the clerk $5, but he gave me change for $20. This was a substantial sum of money to my family in 1946. I knew the clerk had made a mistake, but I said nothing.

When I went home with the extra money I thought I would be rewarded, because I often overheard conversations that money was important. Instead, my mother scolded me and together we returned the money to the grocery store. My mother told the proprietor that I did not understand what I had done by not revealing the error; but she knew that I knew what I had done and lectured me again upon returning home that I should not steal. She never made reference to the Bible or the Ten Commandments in this lecture, but I knew better than to do this again from how my parents spoke and behaved.

Another episode happened one Sunday while walking to church with a friend: he opened the envelope he was supposed to give to the Church and took out the dime to buy potato chips for himself. Two thoughts came to me. First, I knew that opening the envelope on the way to church and not putting it into the collection basket was wrong; that dime belonged to the Church. Secondly, I was struck by the fact that his envelope had a dime and mine only had a nickel.

The third episode concerned food. One day my grandmother made veal cutlet sandwiches for my friend and me to take outside to eat. My friend opened his sandwich and threw the meat away. I immediately understood that throwing the meat away was both disrespectful of my grandmother and wasteful. I felt sorry for my friend because he didn't know better and that he was missing a great sandwich. I also felt cheated that I could not have his sandwich (oh, for one of those sandwiches today). Throwing food away was a sin for sure – my mother and father worked hard to provide food for their family, and my grandmother worked hard cooking as well.

The streets provided me with an education that allowed me to see things differently from what I was exposed to at home, or what I might have learned through formal weekly catechism classes after school.

Moral and religious education came in disjointed fragments on the streets – as did sex education. During the early 1940s, outdoor time presented a freedom to discuss naughty things with male playmates. We read little neighborhood pamphlets referred to as eight pagers. These eight pagers consisted of hand drawn cartoons, and they introduced me to pornography. They were basically comic books that depicted individuals engaged in sexual acts. The drawings were accompanied by commentary enclosed in bubbles over the speaking person's head.

As a youngster my buddies and I viewed the eight pagers with amazement, without fully understand what we were viewing. Neighborhood teenage boys provided the eight pagers. Adults certainly did not know what we were looking at and would have called the eight pagers filth. We did not know the material was filth even as we looked at the drawings and read the words. Nevertheless, we viewed the eight pagers with a naughty delight – if adults only knew! Some of the kids and I eventually did grasp what the pornographic depictions were about.

The term c..k-sucker was often used on the streets by the teenagers. Most of the younger kids did not have a sense of the meaning of the term, other than it was name calling, no different than calling someone stupid or a sissy. I gained status among my buddies when I deciphered the phrase c..k-sucker as an activity. The eight pager was my first reference book. Church on Sundays and eight pagers during the week.

We sang a popular cigarette jingle at that time – LSMFT which was an acronym for "Lucky Strikes Means Fine Tobacco." This referred to the Lucky Strikes brand of cigarettes, commonly referred to as Luckies, and the jingle was sung on radio commercials. Teenage boys changed the jingle and sang LSMFT as "Loose Safeties Mean Fat Tummies." Of course, the younger boys (including me) also sang the jingle, though we didn't understand what it meant.[32]

Cold Weather Play

Fall began early in Buffalo, with leaves on the trees changing color close to the official calendar date of autumn, in September. Weather in Buffalo started to become brisk during late September, and by October jackets and sweaters were required. By the end of October, most trees had shed their leaves.

Our neighborhood on Busti had many chestnut trees. These "horse chestnuts" were not edible, but were food for horses, or so I thought. These magnificent trees sprouted many clusters of chestnuts that kids would knock down by throwing sticks at them. The chestnuts would then be turned into play items. We played a game using these chestnuts. The game's objective was to determine who had the hardest nut. Horse chestnuts were attached to a shoelace and swung at another player's chestnut, which was also attached to the end of a shoelace. The person who had the chestnut that was not smashed after being hit by another player's chestnut was considered the winner.

As winter set in there were snowball fights. Snow often fell from early December to mid-March. We always looked for "good packing" snow to make snowballs. Good packing meant that snow was moist and could be molded into a ball that would not fall apart in flight. But if the snow contained too much moisture it was likely to be ice – and being hit with an

---

32 During the war we sang another jingle as well: "Hitler is a meanie, Mussolini sucks his weenie, and they both go to Hell."

ice ball hurt and could cause injury. "Good packing" was the cry of neighborhood kids.

The activity of the day would be throwing snowballs at anything we considered a target. We threw snowballs at each other as we chose up sides. I was never warned about throwing snowballs at other kids during snowball fights. The only caution was to be careful of hitting windows that might break or worse – shattering them and injuring someone.

Throwing snowballs at passing cars and trucks was also frowned upon by my parents. There was also the possibility that the driver would get out of the car and chase the snowball throwers. As kids, if we were chased and caught we would have preferred being reprimanded, scolded or even shaken to being brought home by the driver of the vehicle. Our parents would punish us far more than could an aggrieved driver who was a target of our snowball.

No game we played required store-bought equipment (see the Appendix D for a description of our games; I particularly favored the games we called Relievio and Nip). There was one exception: we did have to buy metal roller skates that were adjustable to our shoe size using a skate key.

Everything I've described occurred before I was nine years old, since when I was 8½ we moved to Grant Street, a couple miles away from Busti Ave. I was quite young, and it is difficult for me to be fully accurate in what I remember as a joyous time. I can't say for sure other kids felt the same way I did about what I described.[33]

While I was not a street kid (as that term is commonly understood), most of my outdoor activities were unsupervised. I suppose I was fortunate not to be injured or harmed in some other way. I suspect one of the cautions in writing about the past is to inflate memories that are pleasant and to highlight how wonderful it was in comparison to what I observe today.

---

33 Kids (actually, informal gangs) kept order through ridicule and following a leadership pecking-order. I was not a bully and more importantly I avoided being bullied, as some kids were. But I did not protect others from being bullied.

I can say with some assurance, though, that without adult supervision my playmates and I made our own decisions about what we did to amuse ourselves. We made our own rules for games, and we figured out how to resolve disagreements about what those rules meant. Adults weren't watching us, and we didn't take our disagreements with other kids home to have our parents resolve them. Even before I was nine years old, I was making decisions and learning how to interact with others without being told how to proceed.

This is not what I see today, either with my own grandchildren when they were younger, or even casually in my current neighborhood in the Baltimore/Washington suburbs. Parenting using hyper-involvement has been well-documented by the media as helicopter parents and even snowplow parents have been the subject of discussion for years now.[34] But even if we take these extreme examples off the table, I wonder what impact contemporary parenting has on today's youngsters' ability to make decisions. What effect does the current prevalence of organized play with adult supervision have on the speed at which children feel comfortable and confident in making decisions in uncertain situations? Are children really using their imagination to make up games when the adults around them can just google something and tell the young ones how to play? Do kids really learn to negotiate with each other when an adult is present to call fair or foul? Certainly, these are all forms of education that need to be encouraged – while still assuring that children are safe from many forms of harm.

The world of Busti Avenue – both inside and outside – was the only world I knew for the first years of my life. But that was all about to change.

---

34 The New York *Times* suggested some of the implications of these parenting styles in the wake of the 2019 college admissions scandal; see https://www.nytimes.com/2019/03/16/style/snowplow-parenting-scandal.html.

CHAPTER 5 :

GRANT STREET... ITALIANS AS A MINORITY

My world changed in December 1946 – a year after WWII ended. There were six Marando children by then, as my twin sisters – Kathleen and Angela – had been born in June. The two bedrooms of our Busti Avenue home were just not large enough for a family of eight. My parents purchased a house at 566 Grant Street, Buffalo. We would now live two miles from 412 Busti Avenue – two physical miles, but a world away.

My parents often told the story about a bird that crapped on my father's head when they viewed the house for purchase. The bird droppings were a sign of good fortune and that the house was destined to be purchased. Some superstition often accompanied my parents' explanation of situations they confronted, such as buying the house on Grant Street, and my getting polio.

They bought the house for $6,000 in 1946, with monthly mortgage payments of $63. The house also had an upstairs flat and a cottage in the back. The upstairs flat and the cottage both had tenants when we purchased the house.[35]

---

35 Our Grant Street house had a cottage in the "back" which was rented out; now we were the landlords and not the tenants. We watched others make a similar journey to our own: our cottage with its very low rent was a good launching pad into the middle class for the two families with children who lived there over the course of my childhood.

My family in 1945. My mother is holding Eugene in her arms. Standing at the front are Benny, Joey and me.

My twin sisters Kathleen and Angela, aged 3 or 4."

More than superstition was at work when my parents bought the house. The rental income was important to meeting our monthly mortgage payments. The rentals became absolutely critical to my parents' ability to keep the house when my father was laid off from work a few years later.

He was without steady work for almost three years; without the rents, we certainly would have lost our home.

The house was also purchased because of its proximity to public transportation. Having a home on or near a city bus line was a necessity for my father to get to work. My family did not own an automobile. Public transportation was how my father got to his job at the Buffalo Flour Mills, located four miles away, on the waterfront.

Much has been written about how so many people moved to the suburbs after World War II; but moving to the suburbs was out of the question for us. Inadequate public transportation and the dearth of available homes with rental property made moving to the suburbs an impossibility. For us, 1946 was a time for balancing family economics and child-raising values with having a job and having the needed rental income to meet monthly expenses.

The yard separating our front house from the back cottage was quite small –no more than 20 feet. In the back yard there was a long chain link fence separating our property from next door. Along the fence was a rose bush that was magnificent in early summer, along with several lilac trees. I did not know much about flowers or trees, but I felt we were fortunate to have rose bushes and lilac trees in our small yard.

Grant Street itself was a busy two-way street and was also a major city bus route; the buses traveled up and down the street, day and night. I quickly got used to the sounds of traffic; I don't remember being bothered by street noise, especially bus engines. The intersection at the end of my block had two bus stops: one stop was for the Forest Avenue bus line, and one for Grant Street route. These two bus routes tied my home to downtown, and later to my high school and to most employment centers of the city. We got along for a decade without an automobile.

The block of Grant Street on which we lived on was predominantly – but not exclusively – residential. Our block was a mix of duplexes and single-family homes, mostly two-story frame houses. Our block also had commercial establishments: two grocery stores, a gas station, and two taverns, one at each corner. In addition, only three houses down from ours was a small factory that manufactured and sold hand tools. Past the next five houses in the other direction was an auto collision shop. This part of Grant Street was hardly an idyllic urban lane.

A few blocks further south, Grant Street became a commercial thoroughfare. There were five-and-dime stores, banks, restaurants, jewelry establishments, clothing stores, bakeries, movie theaters, and a variety of other retail establishments. And there was a tavern at almost every corner for the entire length of Grant Street.

At the end of my block was an ice cream parlor with a soda fountain. It looked much the same as you might see in contemporary movies about the late '40s and early '50s. The proprietors were an older couple named Nick and Polly, after whom the ice cream parlor was named. I hung out at the ice cream parlor on non-school nights.

One Friday night, I heard Nick say that I must be Catholic. He said that he could smell fish on me. I don't doubt that he did. Fridays meant fish for dinner at my house. When we moved to the neighborhood, it signaled a change in the customers that would frequent the ice cream parlor. I can imagine Nick and Polly thinking, "Who are these Catholics and Italians no less?" Nick never said anything else after this comment. What he said did not alter my frequent visits to his ice cream parlor. I suppose we came to understand one another over time. Throughout my elementary and high school years I visited Nick and Polly's frequently.

Our house at 566 Grant Street was a large, three-story structure: it was the tallest house on the block. It had a basement (which we called a cellar), two flats, and an attic. Our property also included a four-room cottage in the back of our house. Our basement was dark, with a bin for storing coal from which to feed our furnace throughout Buffalo's long winters. Of course, the coal bin had to be refilled from a truck that delivered to the curb in front of our home. I assisted my father in shoveling coal into the cellar coal bin through a basement window each fall and winter. More than one delivery of coal was needed most winter seasons to heat our home. As Benny and I grew older, we shoveled the coal into the cellar on our own, after school. My father replaced the coal furnace with a natural gas furnace a few years later.

The cellar was cold, dark, and damp most of the time. It was not one of my favorite places to play. The cellar contained a five-foot long, two-foot wide, rectangular tool chest that I thought resembled a coffin. I was fearful of getting into the "coffin" during games we played in the cellar. Benny was braver than me. He would get into the chest and jump out to frighten unsuspecting neighborhood kids we invited to our cellar.

Although our home was a formidable structure, it was not as large inside as it appeared from the outside. The house sat on a 5-foot rise that made it look taller and more substantial than it was. The house was built in 1910, and it was drafty – there were no storm windows to keep out the cold winter wind. Our home had three bedrooms, a kitchen, a dining room and front room, which we called the parlor.

Still, the house was far from ideal for raising six young children: it had a single bathroom which was shared by my parents and all of us kids. Our new home increased the number of bedrooms to three, which was better, but remained a challenge for housing my family. I still shared a bedroom with two brothers. At first my brother Eugene and the twins shared the third bedroom. As the twins grew older and needed their own room, the four boys shared a single bedroom containing two "three-quarter size" beds – that meant three-quarters of a standard-size double bed. The four of us shared a single closet. We each had one drawer of a dresser which contained our underwear, socks and polo shirts. The sleeping arrangements were better than Busti Avenue, but we were still cramped.

Our house sat only 10 feet from the street. The "front yard" (if you could call it that), was on a sloping "hill" and not fenced off from the street. This was not safe or appropriate as a play area. But no one in my family, over the years, was ever injured by a vehicle – all the Marandos understood that we lived on a busy street and were careful of traffic at all times.Our house had an attic with a creaky wooden floor, exposed beams and no insulation. However, I enjoyed the attic much more than the cellar. The attic was empty, except for a few old travel trunks left over from the previous owner. A few of the newspapers lining the storage trunks dated back to the turn of the century. Most of the newspapers lining the trunks contained more recent newspapers from the 1930s and 40s. Some of the newspaper articles reported World War II air battles over London; one photo showed British Hurricane fighter planes battling the German Luftwaffe over England. At the moment I found them, those newspapers were only six years old. Yet, it felt like the newspapers were historical markers – which they were. The photos stimulated my interest in studying the past, particularly the Second World War.

With no insulation, the attic was cold in the winter and hot during the summer. During the summer I would seek a window at the front or back of the attic to feel a cool breeze of fresh air. From the rear window there was a magnificent view of the neighborhood, the Erie Canal and the Niagara River. Lake Erie narrowed and flowed into the Niagara River and Erie Canal about a mile from my house. The Erie Canal ran along the shore (separated by the break wall from the river), then turned inland until it connected with the Hudson River 300 hundred mile to the east. From my attic the view of the canal and river was magnificent and inspiring.

The place where Lake Erie flowed into the Niagara River, near the Peace Bridge, was referred to as "the confluence." Confluence was one of the first big words I learned and understood. I did not learn the word at school, but through the experience of hearing others use it. I could actually see the confluence of Lake Erie and the Niagara River whenever I crossed the Peace Bridge, going to and from Canada.[36]

A Cultural Divide

In 1946, it wasn't unusual for Italians (and for my family in particular) to relocate from one part of the city to another to obtain better housing. My family was among the very first to move to the Grant and Forest area. Although our house on Grant Street was only two miles from 412 Busti Avenue, I felt there was a massive cultural divide between the two neighborhoods. One was predominantly Sicilian, and the other was an ethnic mix including Irish, Germans, Polish – and, of course, few Italians. My new neighborhood was white and working-class. There were many kids whose ethnicity I could not Identify; I referred to them as Americans. In retrospect, it seems strange that I would feel like a minority when I moved from living among Italians on Busti Avenue. With Non-Italians and Protestants around me, I had moved to a different America.[37]

Social class, more than ethnicity, defined the area. If there was discrimination against Italians, the reason was that we had "funny" last names. Some of us, especially me, looked different with my black curly hair. By 1951 – five years after we moved – other Italians started locating to the area. Joe Di Geralimo (the kid with the bullets from Busti Avenue) moved three blocks from our home. Joe also attended PS52 – my school.

---

36 Occasionally I walked over the Peace Bridge to Canada with other neighborhood kids to buy fireworks, which were not legal for purchase in New York State. More often I walked over the Peace Bridge with my father to visit his Italian cousins, Vincent and Joseph Marando, who lived in Fort Erie, Canada. They were not allowed to immigrate directly into the United States; instead they immigrated to Canada before seeking and gaining entrance to the United States.

For several years in the early 1950s my father and I would take (actually, smuggle) American cigarettes to Vincent and Joseph. Canadian cigarettes were not the same quality and were more expensive than American cigarettes. When we visited them on Sundays, taverns and drinking establishments were not open to the public. That didn't stop my father and his cousins from drinking beer, which was provided by the boardinghouse owner from whom they leased their rooms. The three Italians would be in the basement drinking Canadian beer: the law could only go so far in keeping individuals from their beer, even on Sundays.

37 I never thought about walking the 2 miles between Grant Street and Busti Avenue. That distance seemed beyond my ability to walk when I was a grammar school student. I did not own a bicycle.

In 1953, Salvatore "Sam" Incardona moved from the deep West Side to a house a few doors down from ours. There was a changing social mix in the neighborhood, with more and more Italians moving to the Grant-Forest area. Although Italians remained a minority, I no longer felt isolated.

There were Protestants as well as Catholics living in my new neighborhood. I did not recognize Protestants before moving to Grant Street. The difference between Catholics and Protestants was a big difference to me. (I was not aware of the presence of any Jews or people of any non-Christian faith in my neighborhood.) Most of the Catholics in the area were Irish or Polish, who were generally more light-skinned than Italians. They were not noticeably different from Protestants in appearance. The Irish kids attended the Catholic Annunciation Church five blocks to the South. The Polish kids attended Assumption Church six blocks to the north, in the heavily Polish Blackrock area.[38]

The neighborhood was safe. If there was conflict, it was manifested mostly in name-calling and minor scuffles among kids, but we generally got along with one another. Discrimination was expressed mostly by name-calling, with little understanding by the name-callers of what being Catholic meant, other than someone who ate fish on Friday and was led by a Pope who lived in Rome. Being referred to as a "Catlick" was about as ugly as it got. A couple of years later, we were accepted residents in the neighborhood.

The Irish Smyth family – who first lived in our cottage and later moved next door when a larger house became available – attended Annunciation Catholic Elementary School, six blocks away. My parents were not interested in having their children attend a Catholic elementary school: PS52 was on the next block and was where I and my brothers and sisters attended school. Catholic schools charged a modest tuition to attend – any tuition was not acceptable to my parents as long as a "free" public school was nearby.

---

38 There were no African-American families living in my new neighborhood when we moved in 1946. A few African-American families moved into to the area in the mid-1950s; all the kids attended PS52.

Our family was committed to public schools for our education. The reasons were largely about cost – our parents were not particularly fearful that we would miss out by not receiving a Catholic education from nuns. Catholic students were released from PS52 on Tuesday afternoons to attend catechism classes for one hour each week. This was adequate exposure to religious education for my brothers, sisters and me.

There was a moment when this was tested, though. My younger brother Eugene, six years younger than me, was enrolled in a Catholic school for one year, when he was not promoted at PS52. My parents thought a Catholic school would provide him a better education. It did not. He returned to PS52 the next year.

After the first year and a half of living on Grant Street (when I entered the fifth grade as a ten-year-old), my mother and father allowed me to return to Busti Avenue on weekends – *by myself*. I was a responsible kid, but I suspect that having one child away for the weekend was a gift to my parents as well as a great opportunity for me to be independent.

I left after school on Friday afternoons to spend the weekend with my friends from the old neighborhood. I was given the freedom to stay the weekend at my grandparents' home. I was allowed to take the Grant Street Bus to visit my old neighborhood on Busti Avenue. In fact, Busti was a world which was difficult for me leave – a world I was happy to recreate on weekends. I would return home to Grant Street with my family, after Sunday dinner with my grandparents.

I slept in my Uncle Buddy's bed, in the room he ostensibly shared with my Great Uncle Sam. I felt fortunate that my Uncle Buddy rarely used his bed, although he had not formally moved out. I do not recall a single instance when he came home and slept in that bed. As I think back on my uncle's empty bed, I remember that my grandparents never spoke openly of where he spent his nights; they kept referring to the room as Buddy's bedroom, never confronting the fact that he did not live at home anymore.

There were rumors that Buddy slept at home on occasion – but I never saw him sleep there.

Buddy was handsome, resembling the 1940's movie matinee idol Clark Gable. He was what was referred to as a sharp dresser. I assume he never had problems attracting women. Buddy was not married at the time, and never did marry, although he lived with various girlfriends. I am not certain whether the girlfriends lived with him in his apartment, or he lived in their homes or apartments – this was not a topic spoken of in front of me.

When I stayed overnight on weekends, I shared Buddy's bedroom with my Great Uncle Sam, my grandmother's brother.[39] I suppose the bedroom was more my great Uncle Sam's than Buddy's, but that wasn't how it was identified. Uncle Sam was in his early 60s when I began staying overnight on weekends. Sam was a bachelor who always seemed old, odd and eccentric. He had few friends, either male or female. No one ever expected him to get married. I never saw him with women or with someone considered to be a girlfriend, but I don't think he was gay. Sam was, quite possibly, an alcoholic. I thought of him more as a kind old soul, eccentric and a hermit. He was just part of the family, and no one questioned it.

Sam was a United States Army World War I Veteran who never stopped reliving his war experiences and singing World War I songs, particularly after he drank wine. Sam was part of the U. S. Calvary and cared for horses at an Army base in New Jersey. Yes, the Army relied on horses in World War I. He never ventured anywhere closer to France – or combat – than the U.S. East Coast. [40]

My grandparents provided Sam with a home from the time he immigrated to the United States before the Great War (WWI) in 1914. My

---

39 Uncle Sam was the person not reported in the 1940 U.S. Census. I will never know for sure why Sam was not reported to Gertrude.
40 My grandmother's other brother, Dominic, saw combat in France during WWI. Dominic was exposed to mustard gas during the war, and I believe he may have been awarded the Purple Heart (no one ever mentioned receiving the medal.) Dominic's son, Russell "Rosario" entered the Air Force in World War II and was shot down by German aircraft ferrying planes across the Atlantic. Russell retired as a full Colonel from the Air Force.

grandfather accepted Sam good-naturedly. I never heard the two of them quarrel or even become disagreeable with one another. My Great Uncle Sam ended up living in the house alone for several years after everyone else had married, died, or gotten their own home.

My family would have dinner at my grandparent's home every Sunday. We did not own an automobile to get to Busti Avenue and taking the city bus was too much for my father, mother, and five children (I was already at my grandparents' house, spending the weekend). My Uncle Russell or my grandfather would drive to Grant Street to bring my family for dinner.

I rode back home with my family after dinner, which made the car crowded with nine of us – my family as passengers and my grandfather as the driver. We would often stop at Christiano's Bakery near my grandfather's house for Italian bread or rolls for the next day's school and work lunches. Grant Street did not have Italian bakeries at that time, as it would years later when more Italians had moved to the area.

Life in My New Neighborhood

Although Grant Street had heavy traffic and homes had small backyards, there were many areas within walking distance in which to play and explore. In the late 1940s and early 1950s, also within walking distance (about a block and a half from home) was PS52, my elementary school.[41] Our elementary school had an asphalt playground. The playground was not an ideal place to play, yet I played there often with neighborhood kids.

Just one city block from my home was a major New York State psychiatric facility, on Forest Avenue housing well over 600 patients in the late 1940s and early 50s. As a young kid, I referred to the facility as the "Crazy House" or "Forest Avenue." Buffalo State Teachers College ran alongside this psychiatric facility, just a block away in the other direction. The two

---

41 In my neighborhood a city block was between 150 and 200 yards in length. I do not recall a single school that bussed children to attend; all grammar schools were within walking distance for students to attend.

state facilities occupied a square mile of the inner city, much of which was open space – and all within a short walking distance of my home.[42]

The large grassy areas of these state facilities were often used as play-fields for neighborhood kids. Of course, the grassy areas in the psychiatric facility were fenced – but these were easily climbed to gain access to the lawns. The fence was supposed to protect both patients and neighborhood residents, and as kids we were always looking over our shoulders to see if an escaped patient was going to chase us. In all the years I played on the psychiatric facility grounds, there was never an escapee from the hospital. No patient ever escaped — and patients certainly did not want to chase us.[43]

It was not unusual, though, for some patients to be granted day leave to visit family or to go to a nearby large city multi-purpure sports and rec-reation facility on Reese Street. One adult patient was referred to as "Fish" because he was a fast swimmer and was proud of his swimming ability. As a kid I would race Fish at the Reese Street pool. He usually won the races –he was an adult and I was nine or ten years old – but he was a willing com-petitor. I used him as a standard to determine how good a swimmer I was.

Most of New York State's property was committed to Buffalo State College's future expansion. In the late 1940s, the college consisted of four classroom buildings surrounding a quad, with two dormitories and several temporary annex buildings. As a youngster I would run through the cam-pus looking for empty soda bottles to return for the two-cent deposit. (I often thought about those days of scavenging when I attended Buffalo State years later, graduating in 1960.)

---

42 The Buffalo State Hospital (originally called the Buffalo State Asylum for the Insane) was originally built in the late 19th century; land from the hospital was taken for Buffalo State Teachers' College in 1927. New buildings were constructed for the hospital in the 1960s and 1970s; the original buildings have been preserved and are currently being used as the Hotel Henry Urban Resort and Conference Center. Pictures of the buildings as they were when I was a child can be seen at https://opacity.us/site35_buffalo_state_hospital.htm.
43 There were additional open spaces close to our Grant Street home. Two blocks away was a large city recreation area and public swimming pool. Beyond the pool was non-psy-chiatric open space committed to the state's future growth needs. This open space was unfenced; we roamed and played there without fear of trespassing.

Behind the college was the City's public Reese Street Recreational complex. This "playground" contained baseball diamonds, tennis courts, one-wall handball courts, and a large aquatic facility consisting of three pools. One pool was a regulation Olympic-sized 50-meter outdoor pool. Another pool was a diving pool that was 12 feet deep and had six diving boards ranging in height from 1 to 3 meters. There was also a third pool that I referred to as the "baby pool," though it was officially a wading pool.[44] The pools were open from the end of June after the school year ended until Labor Day – a two-month swim season.

Extending a mile further east from my home was Delaware Park, designed by Frederic Law Olmstead. The park was magnificent, with a lake that had rowboats for rent during the summer and ice skating during the winter. It was also home to the city zoo and a public golf course.

Delaware Park had also been the site the 1901 Pan-American Exposition – at which President William McKinley had been assassinated. Two of the original buildings from the Pan American Exposition remained as part of Delaware Park's treasures. These two buildings, of Greek and Roman design, had been refurbished and were placed on the National Historical Register. One building housed the Buffalo and Erie County Historical Society (BECHS), while the other was home to the Albright-Knox Art Gallery. I found these historical institutions to be great educational resources, and I spent much time exploring the art collections and roaming among the antiquities in the historical building. There was no admission charge to enter either building and both remain to this day.

I was never questioned by my parents as to how far I went to play and explore after school. As was common among most families at that time, there was relatively little supervision of grade school children during play hours. If I came home dirty, wet, or muddy, I might have been reminded about not getting dirty the next time I went out to play. And that was about it.

---

44 In 1955, I became a lifeguard at this swimming pool and I later became manager of the aquatic facility.

All these play areas, recreational facilities, state institutions, historical institutions and even an art gallery were within easy walking distance from my home. I came to think I was fortunate to live on Grant Street – after I had acclimated to my new neighborhood.[45]

After we moved to Grant Street, I attended PS52, a kindergarten through eighth grade school (K-8). I began attending in the 3rd grade. My adjustment to the new school and classmates was slow with no memorable issues of fitting in, either positive or negative. Due to entering class midyear as we moved in December, I had to make up work missed because of the transfer. Surprisingly, what caught my attention more than having to make up missed work was that PS52 had desks that were mobile and could be moved into different seating arrangements. The desks at PS1 (my former school) had been bolted to the floor in a straight line. I felt I was attending a more modern school than I had been.

PS52 was a large school with over 900 students. All students walked to school – no more than four blocks from all directions. The school's boundaries included a range of families, mostly working class, but some from the middle-class, and some lower incomes kids. There were even a small number of families who were prosperous small business owners: Nicky Del Bello's father owned and operated a mortuary, and Mary Svenson's father owned a jewelry store on Grant Street that made PS52's graduation rings. I recall when Mary brought the rings to school for the kids who had ordered them, I did not have money to complete the $9 purchase, yet she gave me the ring with the promise that I would pay later – which I did. I was surprised that she trusted me to pay her later.

---

45 See Appendix B for my contrast of Buffalo neighborhoods with Tim Russert's depiction of Buffalo from his book, *Big Russ and Me* (2004).

PS52 as it looked when it was built. A gym and auditorium were added later. The school has since been demolished; a post office sits on the site.

Most kids at PS52 were well-behaved most of the time – though of course there were a few older boys who were rough, tough and intimidating. Teachers generally weren't aware of bullying or other situations where students were being intimidated, but students were monitored by faculty and disciplined when they were caught creating mischief.

On the whole, attending PS52 was a good experience and came to make an important and necessary contribution to my education and personal development. The primary reason was the interest shown by several teachers who recognized my classroom effort, which was more impressive than my actual academic performance.

I don't have any clear memories about how well I did in class after we moved, but at the end of the school year, I was promoted from the third grade to the fourth grade. My brother Benny was not promoted from the second to the third grade. Benny was smart, but he was often too physically active. His teacher may have felt that he did not pay attention. I believe Benny may have suffered discrimination by his teacher for not behaving properly due to his lack of attention. If Benny was in school today, he might be classified as having some form of Attention Deficit Syndrome (ADS) – and possibly Attention Deficit Hyperactivity Disorder (ADHD).

Benny's failure in the second grade was followed by another failure in the third grade. Although we were only one year apart in age his double failure separated us in school by three grades. The increase in class separation affected who were our classmates in school, and it also impacted who we hung around with after school as well.

I have few memories of the fourth grade, but one is indelible: I learned that coconuts had milk in their core and that dates grew on palm trees and were very sweet. I had never seen either a date or a coconut (much less tasted them) – but I was enthralled.

I was also assigned to a weekly remedial speech class grade. I was told that I did not pronounce "S's" properly and had to practice in a weekly speech session with other students (there were few students, no more than eight in the class). The one time I attended that class, I had to repeat many words that had an "S" sound. I believe the teacher, Mrs. Smith, was trying to fill her class with students with whom it was easy to make a case that their speech could be improved. After attending one speech class during the fourth grade, I did not need any further speech therapy, and I never heard anything else about having a "speech impediment." I did not understand – then or at any time later – why I needed speech therapy.

The rest of the fourth-grade year was unexceptional – except that I was promoted (or as was said at that time, "passed") from the 4th grade to the 5th grade "*on condition*." I suppose that meant I entered the fifth grade on probation.

I did not know what "on condition" meant, and I still don't know. Judy Smyth, a neighbor who was about my age who attended Annunciation Catholic School, brought the "on condition" passing status to my attention when she looked at my report card.

My fourth-grade teacher was Mrs. Vicks, who used cough drops often during class. (Mrs. Vicks used cough drops – a coincidence?) My grade average in her class was around 75%, which was the passing grade at that time (letter grades were not used). I suppose that 75% meant I would have been a "C" student. I may have received the equivalent of a "D" in English and spelling.

I received no warning from my teacher that it was possible that I could fail the grade.[46] Nor was there any discussion with my parents about my school performance. My parents did not attend any parent-teacher conferences to discuss or monitor my classroom performance and behavior. My mother would look at my report card when I brought it home, sign it and I would return it to school. My father was not at home during the day to examine my report card. I am not sure my father would have known how to evaluate my school performance. They both considered it most important that I behaved in school.

On quarterly report cards at PS52, along with subject grades, was a grade of "E." That grade was for deportment, which included behavior and effort. A grade of "E" meant I put effort into my schoolwork – and I always received E's on my report card. Looking back, these E's accurately reflected my work as a student as much as my letter grades did. I was attentive and hard-working, and several teachers in later grades interpreted this as scholastic potential.

Fifth Grade, A Very Traditional Teacher, and The Wonder of Reading

Mrs. Kervel was a very traditional fifth grade teacher. She once corrected me when I called her "madam"— she said she was no madam. After that, she was always Mrs. Kervel. She required that students be obedient and listen to her, especially when she read to us each morning after roll call. Her classroom was quiet and orderly.

She assigned each student a personal number for the entire year based upon alphabetical order of our last names; when she wanted us to lineup, we did so by our assigned number. Having an "M" as the first letter of my last name, I was assigned number 10 out of 17 boys. Boys and girls

---

46 Benny's class failures frightened me – I was fearful of failing a grade in school. Failure in school would have been personally devastating and would have remained with me – indefinitely.

would assemble in separate lines by number when leaving the classroom to go anywhere in school, particularly to the gym or the auditorium.[47]

Mrs. Kervel was older than the other teachers at PS52; she had white hair set in a bun, and she often sat at her desk while she taught. I suspect looking back she was not as old as I thought, but she was not a very animated or an engaging teacher. She would read a chapter from a novel to the entire class as the first activity each morning for a half hour. She did not asked students to participate in reading from the novel. She asked students a few questions about what she had read, there was limited class discussion.

During the entire year she read three books to the class while we listened seated at our desks. The first book was *Toby Tyler*, which was about a boy who ran off to join the circus where he learned life lessons as he matured into adulthood.[48]

The second book was also about a young boy who was very wealthy and pampered. While the boy was on a transatlantic ocean liner he fell overboard and was rescued by Portuguese fishermen. The theme of the book was that a wealthy boy had to earn his keep by working with the fishermen. He also learned life lessons and matured while in the care of the Portuguese fisherman who took a fatherly interest in him. This book was Rudyard Kipling's *Captains Courageous*.[49]

The third book Mrs. Kervel read to the class was *Johnny Tremaine*. Johnny Tremaine was a teenager who worked for a silversmith in Boston during the American Revolutionary War. Once again, she had selected a coming-of-age story: a young boy overcoming adversity to become a

---

47 Since the fifth grade, I have been fond of the number ten, after having responded to it for an entire year. I thought number 10 was my "lucky" number, and I still single out the number 10 on the jerseys of football, basketball, baseball and lacrosse players.

48 *Toby Tyler* by James Otis (James Otis Kaler) was originally published in 1881. Disney Studios made the book into a movie in 1960.

49 *Captains Courageous* was originally published in 1897. It became a 1937 motion picture starring Spencer Tracy as the Portuguese fisherman; Tracy won the Academy Award for Best Actor for his performance, and the movie won the award for Best Picture. It was also adapted for television in 1977 and 1996.

Revolutionary War hero.[50] Note that all three books were about boys coming of age not girls.

Fifth grade was not terribly memorable – except for Mrs. Kervel reading three books to our class. I must have enjoyed being read to, because I remember with fondness and in surprising detail the three books from which Mrs. Kervel read. Her teaching method was quite appropriate for what I needed at that time: I became an avid reader after the fifth grade. As an adult, I also take great pleasure in listening to books on tape. Make no mistake, I was not reading the Harvard Classics – I was reading what was available, which was most of the time likely to be comic books, which I truly enjoyed. Maybe for my needs at the time she wasn't such a passive teacher after all.

Over the summer following fifth grade, I made a trade with a neighborhood boy – my soccer ball for a large box of comic books. I think we both felt we got the better deal. I recall learning the word "reasonable" from the comic books. I was surprised that the word was used by two boys who were sorting out how to solve a problem between them. I had never used that word before.

Fifth grade was also the year that I had a 13-year-old classmate named Elton. Elton was older than the rest of the fifth graders, who were all about 10 years old. Elton had failed a previous grade – more than once. Mrs. Kervel understood the circumstance and consequences of Elton being older than the rest of his classmates. Some classmates considered Elton "slow." Mrs. Kervel gave Elton the responsibility of cleaning the blackboard erasers at the end of each day.

Our class had slate blackboards – which were actually black. White chalk was used to write upon the blackboard – which created a great deal of dust. When students went to the blackboard to write, there was quite a mess – dust everywhere, and hands white with chalk. In the hands of most

50 *Johnny Tremaine* was written by Esther Forbes and first published in 1943. The work won the Newbery Medal in 1944 and continued to be popular into the 21st century; it was the 16th best-selling children's book in the year 2000. Disney made the book into a movie in 1957.

children the chalk squeaked and squealed when pressed against the blackboard. As children we were instructed and on how to hold the chalk so it would not squeak and squeal, but few of us mastered the art of noiseless writing on the blackboard.

Elton cleaned the erasers in the "cloak" room;[51] there was a special immobile vacuum cleaner that was bolted to the wall. (The chalk-cleaning machine was kept in the cloak room so that the dust would not contaminate the classroom.) Elton was assigned the task of vacuuming the chalk dust from the erasers into a bag that was attached to the immobile vacuum. The machine made a loud sound (as would a vacuum cleaner) as the erasers were passed over an opening where the dust was collected into an attached cloth bag.

I believe Elton was given this the assignment to clean the erasers to provide him with a responsibility and a sense of worth. Elton never got into trouble in the fifth grade.

And in fifth grade there was Sue: she was the girl who all the boys had a crush on. Sue was attractive, smart, and more physically developed than any of the other girls in our class. We made a hand gesture to express our feelings for her – and that was about as close as we came to expressing our appreciation. Sue lived on the next block over from my house, in a modest duplex (even by the standards of our neighborhood). Although her home was small, that was not apparent to me. It was a great home, as far as I was concerned – after all, it was *Sue's* home. (Years later, as I passed her home, I recognized how tight it must have been for her family of five.)

PS52 was turning out to be a wonderful school for me. But my education was about to be put into a higher gear.

---

51 I don't know why it was called a cloak room, no one ever wore a cloak. The cloak room was entered from the classroom by the door and was in effect the closet where we hung our jackets, sweaters and put our overshoes and snow boots during the winter. Each class had its own cloak room; there were no individual lockers.

CHAPTER 6:

SUPERCHARGING MY EDUCATION

While attending PS52 there were two separate activities that had a long-term impact on my development and education: swimming and farm work. Both activities contributed to my becoming a better student – and combined with the assistance of some interested teachers, led me to believe I had the potential to be an outstanding student. Both gave me a newfound appreciation for school – increasing my self-confidence and my ability to define and achieve goals. I would actually say that both of these out-of-classroom activities completely changed my academic life – they *supercharged* my education.

Swimming: Preferred Post-Polio

I was encouraged to swim not long after I returned from the hospital as a polio patient. Swimming was considered a necessary therapy for many people who had contracted polio; swimming was something I could do with reasonably little effort that would not further injure me.

I was pulled and pushed toward water from an early age. My family encouraged me to swim, believing the exercise would be good for me. I was told that I would not stress myself swimming as I might playing football, basketball or baseball or any non-aquatic sport.[52]

Although I was encouraged to swim, I never saw any of the adults in my family swim or engage in any aquatic activities. My parents never used the public city swimming pools during the summers. My parents would take the family to nearby Crystal Beach in Canada once or twice each summer. None of the adults ever left the beach to swim (my mother and aunts *may* have waded in the water); I do not know to this day if my parents could swim at all.

Growing up as a first-generation working-class Italian, athletics and sports were valued and prized. I could run, but not very fast. I really enjoyed football and wanted to be a football player. Playing basketball was fun and I was a passable player in pickup games. I played football and basketball in the neighborhood well enough not to be embarrassed, but certainly not well enough to compete after elementary school.

Swimming was a recreational activity for most neighborhood kids during the summer. Access to swimming pools was limited both by season and availability; no one in my neighborhood owned a pool. I had access to a public outdoor pool during the two month summer season.

But having had polio meant aquatics. Aquatics meant swimming competition – or so I thought. Being a swimmer was considered being an athlete. If I could not play other sports very well, neighborhood kids would invariably say I was a good swimmer. Swimming allowed me to participate actively in a working-class athletic culture.

I was the Captain of PS52's championship swim team in 1951. I followed up elementary school competition with swimming on the high school team, I swam in college, and continued swimming competitively until my late 70s with the United States Masters Association (USMA).[53]

---

52 I was never actually stopped from engaging in other sports; there was no way that anyone would have prevented me from engaging in rough and tumble activities.
53 I'm considering returning to competitive swimming to compete in my 80s, where most likely I will be the only swimmer in my age group. By showing up and completing the events I register for, I will be the winner. I guess there's something to be said for fortitude.

The PS52 championship remains the highlight of my career as a competitive swimmer. The singular event of bringing a championship trophy to PS52 created a relationship to a sport that has had a consequential impact on my education, professional career, and life.

I was highly motivated to be involved in athletics in some way, but I was not among the best athletes at PS52 – far from it. In Buffalo at that time there was interscholastic athletic competition among elementary schools, in basketball, baseball, track and field, and swimming. PS52 had a number of outstanding athletes who went on to have distinguished college careers.

But even before there was interscholastic competition, there was "gym class", not referred to as physical education. In gym classes we had to wear shorts and sneakers, if we had them. "Street shoes" were not permitted on the gym floor, but many students did not have sneakers. Boys playing in their socks were not uncommon. Our "gym teacher," Mr. Fred Speidel, could see that I had had polio by the difference in size between my right and left calves and feet.

Mr. Speidel was a World War II veteran who was quite physically fit. He was my father's age but looked and acted much younger. He took no guff, let alone "back talk," from anyone. He was my hero, as I believe he was to many of the boys at PS52. I felt he took a special interest in me as an earnest student and an aspiring athlete – but though he knew that there were lasting effects from my having had polio, he never made reference to me as limited or handicapped.

That 1951 championship and my attachment to swimming as a sport was achieved because of the encouragement and guidance of Mr. Fred Speidel. He opened my world to success and accomplishment through competitive swimming. Mr. Speidel was not a swim team coach – he was "just a gym teacher" at PS52. But he did more for me as a swimmer than any of my later swim instructors and coaches. Mr. Speidel was a truly gifted educator – who wore shorts.[54]

I began badgering Mr. Speidel about joining the swim team before I was old enough to be on the team. He said yes, I could be on the swim team, but I had to be in the sixth grade. It was in the sixth grade that elementary students could compete in citywide athletic competition, which included most of the city's 81 public elementary schools.[55]

It still amazes me that PS52 had a swim team which won a city championship – *without having a swimming pool*. Some of Buffalo's elementary schools did have swimming pools – PS1, my previous elementary school, had a pool. Kids at PS52 who were interested in swimming during the school year would have to walk to a neighboring school – PS56, which was a mile away – to use its pool.[56]

And once we got there, conditions were hardly ideal. Our use of the pool was limited to one hour of practice on Friday afternoons, after school hours. The available time was actually less than one hour, given our travel time and that PS 56 closed at 5pm; by the time we had changed out of street cloths, showered and changed back, our swim session was no more than 45 minutes. In addition, PS56's pool was not the regulation-sized 20-yard pool in which swim meets were held; this pool was only 15 yards in length. But I saw no problems: the PS56 pool more than met my swimming needs. I looked upon access to the pool as a treasure.

---

54 Mr. Speidel was also Jewish, and I believe this also created a certain kind of bond between us. Now at that time I had no understanding of what being Jewish was, or how being Jewish was different than being Catholic; I don't believe there were any other Jews in my neighborhood, and there was probably not a Jewish student at PS52. But Mr. Speidel was a member of a religious minority, while I was an ethnic minority in a predominantly Anglo school. He most likely recognized me as a fellow member of a minority, with potential which he could develop.

55 I suspect the Buffalo elementary school swimming program was among the nation's leaders in encouraging and facilitating water sports. Buffalo's location on Lake Erie (one of the five Great Lakes), meant that water safety was an important part of the curriculum. I am certain that only a few school districts throughout the nation had competitive swimming programs at the elementary school level at that time, but historical data on the period is not readily available.

56 It didn't occur to me until I started to write that it must've been Mr. Speidel who made arrangements for PS52 students to use the PS56 swimming pool.

I joined the PS52 swim team when I entered the sixth grade. Becoming a member of the team meant telling Mr. Speidel that I wanted to be on the team – there were no "tryouts" since there wasn't a long line of swimmers waiting to qualify for a spot.

In fact, PS52 had three swim teams – despite not actually having a pool. There were "A", "B", and "C" teams for boys of different heights. There was quite a difference in height among boys in the sixth through eighth grades. Having a single team would not have given the shorter, younger and smaller boys much of a chance to participate – let alone compete. The A-Team was for the tallest boys, the B team for the in-between sized boys, and the C team for the shortest boys; I do not recall the actual height guidelines for boys to make a specific swim team. I was on the "B" team.

An Extra Boost

After I joined the PS52 swim team in sixth grade, Mr. Speidel "awarded" me with a Young Men's Christian Association (YMCA) "scholarship" – or at least that's how he referred to the $10 YMCA membership that he provided me. The scholarship allowed me the opportunity to attend the "Y"– which had an indoor regulation-size 20-yard swimming pool. I was absolutely thrilled to be a member of the "Y".

In retrospect, I realize what an amazing move this was on Mr. Speidel's part. For a period of several years I was a member of two swim teams: the PS52 team and the Downtown YMCA team. I had a head start in competitive swimming over most of the other boys at PS52 and most other city public elementary school kids. Mr. Speidel must have been confident that I would not only use the scholarship, but I would work hard to become a better swimmer – which I did. He provided me encouragement, an opportunity and support to engage in a sport in which I could succeed. The key for Mr. Speidel was my motivation, not my ability. He saw to it that I would have the opportunity to be a swimmer.

I now believe that Mr. Speidel was an entrepreneur – he knew how to make an investment in kids that would make a difference and pay lasting dividends. That YCMA "scholarship"— in fact a $10 membership – had a major impact on my life by allowing me to become a good swimmer. Where did the funding come from for the scholarship? Only Mr. Speidel knew. He never said how he obtained my membership; he may have paid it out of his own pocket. Although I exhibited no special talent, he made an investment in me, encouraging and guiding me – without knowing how well I would swim.

Entrepreneur was not a term used to describe educators (and certainly not gym teachers) in the late 1940s and early 1950s; yet I think of Fred Speidel as the most gifted entrepreneur with whom I have ever come into contact.

I went to the "Y" on Saturdays and other non-school days; I took the #3 Grant St. bus by myself, traveling to downtown Buffalo, several miles from my home. I had an opportunity to use an indoor pool year-round; this was also my first interaction with an organization that exposed me to Christian values outside my home and the Catholic Church.

At the "Y" I met boys from all parts of the city who were swimmers – we swam together as members of the same team. Swim meets were usually held on Saturdays. I won several ribbons at swim meets over the course of three seasons. If the ribbons I was awarded had been gold medals they would have not been any more valuable to me.

With the extra instruction, practice and wider perspective on life, I matured more aware of the world around me. When I received membership at the "Y," I swam well enough to be among the best swimmers at PS52 by the end of the seventh grade. I dedicated myself to being the best swimmer possible at PS52. That was enough for Mr. Speidel to continue supporting me.

Trouble on the Bus

One day, after our team had completed a Friday practice at PS56, several swimmers, including me, took a city bus to return home. Some of us (about a dozen) got rowdy on the ride home: we shouted, screamed, and hollered, both in the bus and out the windows at passersby. The bus driver told us to keep quiet and behave. We ignored him. He then locked the bus doors so that none of us could leave.

The bus driver drove us all to a local Buffalo Police Department precinct. He stopped the bus and honked the horn until several police officers responded. We were marched into the police station where we had to stand at attention while the police sergeant read us the riot act. And then, of course, the Buffalo P.D. provided Mr. Speidel and the principal of PS52 – Mr. Park – with a report, including our names.

The following Monday morning, both Mr. Speidel and Mr. Park read us another riot act, stressing one possible consequence for our actions: the swim team would be disbanded if such behavior ever was repeated. I was horrified: if the PS52 swim team was disbanded for whatever reason, my swim career would have been over before it started.

As I look back on the lecture given to us by Mr. Park and Mr. Speidel what I remember most was that it was effective: the swim team's behavior never reverted back to any kind of disruption. In part, the swim team exhibited better behavior because only those boys who were truly interested in swimming remained. Students who were there only for recreational swimming did not return after the bus incident. And there were never any reoccurrences of truly bad behavior during my three years on the PS52 swim team.

I do not actually remember much of the lecture that Mr. Speidel and Mr. Park delivered to us, but that day remains in my mind for another – much less serious – reason. As we all stood in the principal's office being disciplined and threatened, one of the boys in the group farted. Not a loud

fart, so it wasn't immediately clear who was responsible. Eventually, I concluded it was Laverne Barwell. The smell was putrid. More threatening was
that the smell lasted for what seemed to be *forever*. I started to smirk – as
did the other boys. Laverne smiled, knowing he was the one responsible,
and he was so proud to have the longest lasting fart smell up to that time.
He may have set a record under circumstances that were awkward to say
the least. I wonder if Mr. Park and Mr. Speidel also smelled that fart and
wanted to get out of the room as much as I did.

African American Swimmers

PS32 was the premier Buffalo elementary swimming team school in
the early 1950s; the school had a swimming pool.[57] The outstanding swimmer on PS32's team was Ralph Hammond, an African American. He was
the 40-yard backstroke city champion for three years, from 1950 to 1952.
Ralph led his team to the city championship in 1950 and again in 1952.
In between those two championships, PS52 won the "B" city swimming
championship.

PS32's entire swim team was African-American; though I've done
some inquiry, I haven't found any other large city in the U.S. that at that
time that had a swim team exclusively composed of African-Americans –
much less one that won a city-wide championship. PS 52's team was made
up of working-class boys, but we all were white. Working-class white boys
as city swim champions was unusual in itself; the competition between our
two schools was truly a rare moment in the history of Buffalo competitive
swimming. PS32 swimmers prevailed in two out of three competitions:
access to facilities, equipment and coaching made a difference for achiev-
ing success – and it still does.

After finishing grade school Ralph Hammond – PS32's best swimmer – and I became teammates at Buffalo Technical High School. We

---

57 A few years later I realized that PS32 was located across the street from Buffalo
Technical High School (Tech), where I attended high school. The Tech swim team practiced
at PS32.

practiced at the PS32 pool – but even together, we were not able to bring a City Championship to Tech.

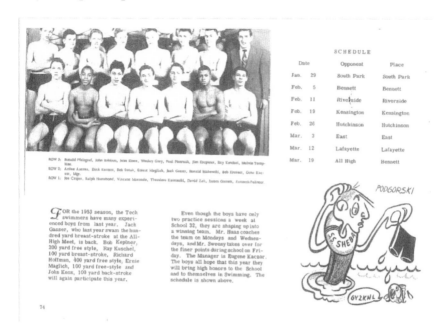

A photo of the Buffalo Tech High School yearbook swim team page. In the front row, Ralph Hammond is sitting second from left and I am next to him, on the right.

Mr. Speidel honored me by selecting me to be the captain of the 1951 PS52 "B" swim team; we went on to be city champions. In the official school photo of the championship team, he placed me in the center; there I was on the front steps of the school, holding the Buffalo City Championship Cup surrounded by my teammates. Mr. Speidel is in the photo on the left and the aforementioned Mr. Park, school principal, on the right. The 1951 swim team photo hangs in my den to this day as a significant tribute to an educator and his legacy to me. Being the captain of that team is still a "wow" moment for me.

The 1951 PS52 Championship Swim Team.

In addition to being captain, I was also the anchor swimmer of the four-person freestyle relay team. The anchor is the last person to swim – and is also considered the fastest swimmer. This was also a tremendous honor.

When I was in the eighth grade, we did not win the city championship again. However, I took second place in the All-City Swim meet in the individual 40-yard breaststroke event. Many teachers and students congratulated me on my second-place medal. I was disappointed that I did not win the gold medal, but I treasure that silver medal to this day.

One of the major benefits I received from swimming was that I did not smoke cigarettes. Smoking even in the seventh and eighth grades was a rite of passage for many boys to show they were becoming adults – but I was "exempt" from that requirement. For some odd reason, there was an expectation that swimmers should not smoke – smoking was considered to reduce your lung capacity. There wasn't any concern at that time about cancer. I don't know if there was any public scientific evidence at the time to support a contention about lung capacity. All I knew was that serious swimmers did not smoke – so I never smoked cigarettes. It was more acceptable, even in my neighborhood, for swimmers not to smoke while the other kids I hung around with did smoke.

As a member of the Buffalo YMCA I visited Camp Weona for one day. Weona was a summer camp in a rural area near Buffalo. I did not know that such nature centers existed. I swam in a small lake for the first time. I swung from a tree vine-actually a rope-into the lake as I imagined Tarzan would. One day at a summer camp- the memory remains vivid. There was more than swimming that I learned being a member of the "Y" then I realized at the time.

Another benefit of swimming came as a result of the "Y" membership that Mr. Speidel awarded to me; as member of the "Y" swim team, I associated with middle-class boys who were different from the boys in my neighborhood. The boys on the "Y" swim team aspired to be on a high school swim team and were likely to go on to college. I was now a part of a new peer group that was interested not only in swimming, but in school as well. Attending college was discussed at practices; swimming was a way of gaining better access to higher education.

Ultimately, swimming did not make a difference in my being able to attend college. There was no tuition at Buffalo State College, where I pursued my undergraduate degree several years later. And ironically, the Buffalo State swim team was in need of swimmers. As in elementary school, showing up for the college's swim team was all I had to do. But those discussions at swim team practices made me aware of one of the ways that swimming could enhance my education.

Winning the city championship had a great impact on me being successful in other realms. Other than swimming, I was not outstanding in any other sport or athletic activity. As I look back, I was not an outstanding swimmer; just good enough among grade schoolers to be among the best. But I took swimming seriously. I believe I may have been the hardest worker among the group. Most of the other elementary school boys on the swim team were more interested and engaged in other sports, such as basketball, baseball and football.

Competitive swimming provided me with confidence and a linkage to engage in many life-altering activities, including going on to college and graduate school and becoming a university faculty member. Mr. Speidel was critically important to this: he recognized that swimming could be an activity that would aid me in overcoming the physical limitations that were the legacy of polio, and he encouraged me to see how swimming could be a centering lifelong activity. This has proven to be true as swimming has been with me my whole life. To this day, I work out swimming laps several times a week.

Gowanda: Another Big Step Toward Maturity

The importance of the year 1951 in my life really can't be overstated. After PS52 won the City Swimming Championship, my father was laid off; he had not been without employment since he took a job with the Buffalo Flour Mills in 1941. He had not – ever – been unemployed during my life. He was a hard worker who gave an honest day's work for his pay. Working to support his family defined him as much as anything else.

My father worked at The Buffalo Flour Mills, a division of the Pillsbury Corporation, which was based in Minneapolis, Minnesota. In 1951, the Buffalo plant was shut down to consolidate operations in Minneapolis. I overheard family discussions about management and labor problems which contributed to closing the Buffalo plant. My father was a valued worker and was asked by plant management to relocate to Minneapolis. He declined the offer to relocate, even though he would be unemployed with a wife and six children.

Relocating for employment would not have been a new experience for my father. He had emigrated from Italy 22 years earlier for the opportunities offered in the United States – including, and especially, finding work.

After arriving in New York City, he later moved to Buffalo when the company he had been working for obtained a contract to construct sewer lines.

But moving to Minneapolis would have been like moving to the moon for my mother and me. All of my mother's lifelong friends lived in Buffalo. But most important was family – our extended family was tightly knit. My mother's ties to her family – the Gardos – were unshakable, and those ties trumped keeping any job if it meant relocating to Minneapolis.

What followed after my father was laid off was temporary and part-time employment for the next three years. Unemployment was a family crisis that I had little understanding of at the time. Even though I was the oldest, I was still under the New York State legal working age of 14.

Only in retrospect did I grasp the consequences and the importance of how we dealt with the unemployment crisis.

My parents did not talk about the impact of my father being out of work in front of me. As the oldest of our six kids, I was the only one to understand some of the implications of unemployment. I certainly did not grasp the full impact of my father being "out of work." I did not overhear much in my parents' conversations, or discussion with anyone else, as to what would come next. I don't know what it would've taken for my father to get a new job as a 42-year-old unskilled laborer in 1951. He had no craft; he possessed only a third-grade education and spoke broken English. He was not a self-promoter. Interviewing for a job would have been a challenge for him.

But my father was a strong, tireless, physical laborer all his life. He had seemingly endless endurance – having never missed a day of back-breaking work at the flour mill.

I remember that a city social worker came to our house to examine where we lived and to assess the value of our house and household items; I never knew the results of the evaluation. One of my parents (most likely my mother) must have contacted the social services agency. I suspect the visit was part of the process of receiving public assistance. I don't believe we ever received public assistance, but I can't categorically swear to that. Entering a social welfare program was not information my parents would have shared with me (or with anyone else, for that matter).

So, my father had to get work and he did – sort of. He did not get a permanent full-time job for three years. His jobs were part-time, seasonal or temporary — "odd jobs." We got by.

I vividly recall a part-time job my father had during the winters, checking fire hydrants to make sure that they weren't frozen. He had a route of several dozen fire hydrants into which he would stick a long pole to determine if the water was frozen. The city public works supervisor then required a report on the condition of fire hydrants. The report consisted of listing every fire hydrant's location by street address or intersection, and whether the hydrant was frozen or not. The report was not difficult to complete, yet my father was unable to write the report due to his language barrier. I wrote the report each day during my lunch hour from elementary school. I was pleased to write the report, feeling that it was a contribution to my family's financial circumstances.[58]

During the years of 1951-1954, my parents did their best to shield us kids about the economic conditions which fostered their insecurity and uncertainty about what was to come next. Although the situation was unsettling, I did not feel it was a threat to our family or to me; we would get through this hardship one way or another. Details about how and where income was to be earned were not held in my presence. I only learned after the decision was made that we were to go to a farm to earn money picking strawberries and beans. We were not going into greater debt! My mother

---

58 Three years later (in 1954), my father did obtain a permanent job with the Buffalo Public School System as a custodian/janitor/coal furnace fireman. The fireman's duties were to keep the coal-fired boiler in a public school operating during Buffalo's long winters; this meant shoveling coal into the furnace and removing the ashes daily, which involved heavy lifting and hot, dirty work. During the fall and spring his duties were those of a custodian (what was often called a janitor). A year after he got the job with the schools, he got a second full time job with the City of Buffalo's Sanitation Department. He worked two full-time jobs for 20 years, until he turned 65. When he retired in 1975, he received social security payments and a city pension of $375 a month.

and father had decided our family would seek the available employment to earn income on which to live, or as was said, to "make ends meet."

And this is the central memory I have of this time period: how we as a family worked together near Gowanda, New York, to earn income and survive my father's unemployment. This is where Gowanda became an integral part of my life experiences of coping with adversity and adapting to change.

Many families living on the Sicilian West Side of Buffalo during the 1940s and early '50s spent summers on what were called "truck farms" south of Buffalo, working as laborers. The work consisted mostly of picking fruits and vegetables that would be shipped to nearby urban areas and canned for national distribution. These farm communities included towns like North Collins, Collins Center, Eden, and Gowanda; Gowanda was the most southern community, and straddled the Erie and Cattaraugus County lines about 35 miles southwest of Buffalo. In 1951, Gowanda was a small town of about 3300 inhabitants (it has since lost about 25% of its population). This area of New York State was known as a fertile truck farming area; working-class city residents provided the farm labor during summers between the closings of schools in June and the reopening in September. I felt no stigma or embarrassment attached to doing farm labor.[59]

In the summer of 1951, my mother – with the six of us kids – spent the first of three summers at Capella's Farm in Gowanda, New York.[60] Gowanda seemed to be a million miles away from everything I knew and the world I had come to understand in Buffalo.

My family arrived at the farm two days after school ended in June and returned to the city two days before the new school year began after Labor Day. We started the work season picking strawberries, and then

---

59 Itinerant immigrant Hispanic agricultural workers (who are often seen today picking farm produce), were not commonly seen in Western New York in the early 1950s.
60 My father remained in Buffalo, working odd jobs and seeking permanent employment. During that period my father also contracted iritis in one eye and had difficulty seeing. He certainly was not capable of reading an eye chart which was necessary for passing a physical for a permanent civil service job which he desired. The infection took the better part of a year to heal. During this period he continued to be intermittently employed.

moved on to raspberries. As the summer entered July, we picked green string beans and yellow wax beans.

I became a farm laborer, prepared to work for an entire summer, which turned into three summers. That first year, my mother was 40 years old, my brother Ben was 11 and I was 13; we were the "workforce." My brother Joe, just 9 years old then, worked on and off, as much as a 9-year-old could be expected to work. The rest of the kids were too young to work; Eugene (age 7) and Angela and Kathleen, "the twins," just 5 years old, played in the fields.

We lived on a farm which was two and a half miles from the Village of Gowanda, not in the village itself. The Capella Farm was on South Quaker Road, outside the town, but we still called it Gowanda. The townies referred to the area as Rosenberg, but it was always Gowanda to me. A farm two and half miles from a village of 3300 residents being considered part of the town is a bit amusing, in retrospect.

Visits by Buffalo relatives were infrequent; no one visited more than two or three times the entire summer, with the exception of my Uncle Russell, and Aunt Rose and Uncle Frank. My family still did not have an automobile and two and a half miles is a long hike up and down the surrounding hills from Capella's farm to travel to the Village of Gowanda. Also, we were expected to work every day, weekends included – unless it rained, or a field was not sufficiently ripe to be picked at that time.

We lived in an unheated, uninsulated, wooden shack for each of the three summers. The shacks (which is what they were actually called) were placed in a row similar to a one-story motel; there were three separate rows of 10 units each. Each shack consisted of two rooms with a wooden slat floor; the two rooms were no more than 15' by 15' each, and there was no indoor toilet or running water or refrigerator.[61] The shacks did have electricity and a natural gas stove for cooking. One of the two rooms was

---

61 One exceptionally large family – the Tebonis – had nine children and a long tenure working on Capella's farm; a singular accommodation was made to provide them an extra bedroom. My family of seven persons – one adult and six children – was not considered unusually large.

a bedroom, and the other an all-purpose room, serving as a kitchen, dining, and living room. A single bed was often part of that all-purpose room when an extra bed was needed, as was the case with my family. Bedroom literally meant bedroom – the two double beds consumed virtually all of the floor space. We appropriated some space behind a curtain as a closet.

That First Night ... and a New Way of Living

I first saw the shacks at Capella's Farm at dusk – after an open truck ride from Buffalo that carried our entire summer's household goods, along with those of several other families. My brother Ben, my cousin Merida (age 14, she would be our "guest" for the entire summer), and I found ourselves on the street, after dark, with our bed and bedding and other household goods – which all needed to be brought into our shack.

All of our household belongings had been dumped in the middle of a dirt road in front of the shack unit assigned to us. The road was dirty and dusty. There was little outdoor lighting, making it difficult to see. The shack had one light bulb in each room which did not illuminate very well. There was an eerie glow inside and outside the shack as well.

Shack #9 was to be our home for the remainder of the summer. The beds had to be assembled and made up with sheets and blankets so that we had a place to sleep.

I don't recall how the three of us brought the household goods inside, especially the beds which had to be assembled with little light by which to see; I think back of that time, my lack of recall is the product of a protective psychological shield. I know I felt like a refugee having to set up camp; my younger brother Benny was looking to my cousin and me for guidance. I am not sure what guidance we offered. We just started to assemble the steel-framed beds.

My mother and the four youngest children would not arrive at Capella's farm until the next day, in my Uncle Russell's pickup truck. Of all my relatives, Uncle Russell visited us most often; he came several times each summer. Uncle Russell was compassionate and generous in his efforts to assist us – he was close to his eldest sister, my mother, whom he looked to for guidance and support. My uncle Buddy did not visit us once during the three summers in Gowanda.

I look back with surprise that my mother had my cousin Merida join us for the entire summer; I had had no idea that Merida was to stay with us that first summer. My mother and my Aunt Grace (Merida's mother) must have worked something out, since six kids, obviously, left plenty of room in a one-bedroom accommodation. We needed an extra person - Ha! Merida got to sleep in the single bed in the kitchen, by herself. The four boys slept in one bed, my mother and the twins slept in the other bed in the same room, with barely enough floor space between the beds for us to get in and out of bed.

A stove with four gas burners was used for cooking. There was also a box of matches by the stove to start the gas burners (always Blue Diamond matches). There was no electric refrigeration so food was kept cold in an ice box. Ice was delivered to our unit once a week by the "iceman." There was also a man who delivered groceries to the farm and he delivered groceries to our shack every few days. He took grocery orders from a number of families that did not have autos. The nearest grocery store was two and a half miles away in the village of Gowanda. This fellow who charged a fee came in a car, not a truck.

We got water for cooking and drinking at a single community spigot in the common space at the end of the rows of shacks. We carried water indoors in kettles and bottles. Fortunately, the outdoor spigot was not too far from our living unit. There were no showering facilities. The outdoor spigot was where we got water to splash upon ourselves to wash after work.

Outhouses, with no running water, served as toilets. There was an outhouse for men and another for women. I can't speak for the women's outhouse, but the men's was a "three hole-er." If there was more than one person using the outhouse, we sat cheek to cheek with no more than a few inches separating those using the facility. I looked down the hole to see where everything went and how the waste would be taken care of. Later I found out that lime was used to cover and disintegrate the waste. There was always an aroma in the outhouse that I got used to after a while. I got used to much that was different, strange, or foreign to my Buffalo lifestyle during that first summer.[62]

Everyone that was at Capella's was part of the working-class, mostly Italian families and we were all on the farm to earn needed income. Although there were differences among the families, all families expected their children who were 10 years old or older to work.

The three of us who worked daily made about $900 for the entire first summer; that averaged out to about $14 a day over a 65-day summer season. We were paid seven cents per quart for strawberries and raspberries, which were early crops picked in late June and early July in Western New York. After strawberries and raspberries had been harvested, we picked mostly green string beans and some yellow wax beans for the remainder of the summer. We were paid two and a half cents per pound for the green and yellow beans. On an exceptionally profitable day, the three of us (my mother, Benny and I) picked 1000 pounds of beans. That meant we made $25 that day. We had very few $25 days.

There were other ways I learned about money, too. I recall listening to a conversation between a boy my age and his father concerning the need for auto insurance – a requirement if one wanted to own and drive a car. With my family not owning a car, and I had no grasp on what it might cost to buy and drive a car, let alone that insurance was needed. They estimated that about $170 was needed to purchase car insurance for a year. I was absolutely shocked that one had to pay that much money each year to insure a car – on top of just purchasing it and buying gasoline, not to

62 New cinderblock buildings were constructed two years later, in 1953. These facilities included running water, toilets, and shower facilities. The new buildings had hot and cold running water, flush toilets, and showers. These modern facilities – one for men and one for women— were a welcome luxury that made it possible to take showers after work.

mention providing for maintenance, such as replacing worn out tires. I figured I would never have enough money to own a car.

Looking back at my experience on the farm, none of what I describe seemed unusual at the time. I did not think we were actually poor, but on the farm for a reason, if not a mission. A number of families were in the same circumstance. We all saw ourselves as in similar situations, and no one was being treated differently than the others. We were part of a community with a common purpose: to make a living and keep families together. Overriding all my circumstances, which may look dire by today's standards, was the realization at the time that this condition was not permanent. Gowanda was a stage that was necessary for my family and others as well, as we moved forward from our current environment to what we hoped would be better economic conditions. A work ethic was imbued in most of us that remained with everyone I have come into contact with from Gowanda since that time.

Several of the kids at Capella's (all of us in our early teens at that time) went on to get college degrees, pursuing careers in various professions. This obviously included me. Two boys – one my age and his younger brother – went on to get appointments to the U.S. Naval Academy at Annapolis. They had distinguished naval careers. Both of these boys, as well as their younger sister, were valedictorians of their class at Grover Cleveland High School on Buffalo's West Side.

Everyone who worked on the farm knew that these three children were academically gifted. I stumbled upon a conversation that the two brothers were having with their father at the end of a row of shacks. The three were discussing and singing the novelty tune "Mairzy Doats," which remained popular a decade after it was written and played over the radio. In their discussion they deciphered the song. I was familiar with the song, as were many kids at that time. I did not know what words of the song meant; or if the words meant anything at all except jazzy scat phrases that could be sung by persons who were tone deaf – such as me. I thought it was just a catchy string of nonsense words strung together to be sung by all who heard it – until the discussion among the three brought to my attention that the song not only rhymed in a nonsensical way, but also that the words had meaning.

The catchy phrase was "Mairzy doats and dozey doats and little lamzy divey, and kiddley divey too, wooden shoe." I understood by their discussion that the words meant "mares eat oats, and does eat oats, and little lambs eat ivy, [a] kid will eat ivy too, wouldn't you?"

This was a critical moment for me: the boys and their father provided me with a lesson on how to listen closely and make sense out of what was actually being communicated by the song. After a whole summer's work I learned the meaning behind the Mairzy Doats jingle, as well as contributing to my family's income. The skill remains, the jingle remains – the income is long gone.

I also got a few tips about being courteous and polite from the same family. On one occasion the same family invited me as a guest to go with them by auto to Gowanda for ice cream. I entered the back seat of the car first and sat by the nearest window. The next passenger had to climb over me to the middle seat. I was gently reminded that I should have moved to the other side of the seat, so those who followed me would not have to climb over me. This was a small but a memorable lesson.

I learned a very different kind of etiquette lesson from Joey Combo. Joey was from a large family who occupied two separate housing units. One of the units consisted only of a couple of beds that he and his brother would use. One evening he invited me over to his unit to share his treasured peephole between his shack and the one next door. The peephole allowed us to see an older teenage girl undressing in the next shack. She was probably 17; Joey and I were 13. We took turns peeping through the knot in the pine plank wall separating the units. We had to be quiet as we nudged and pushed each other to get a longer, better view. Her room was not well lit, but we could see the silhouette of her body, especially her breasts. Joey invited me only for that one viewing – he kept the peephole to himself for the rest of the summer. I should have realized that I was Joey's guest and a peephole meant a peep —not watching a movie.

I was coming-of-age on a farm. I was experiencing a broader world from different perspectives – even when confined as a field laborer all day, every day for the entire summer.

We were awakened each morning a little bit after 6 o'clock by a woman ringing a cowbell. She had been associated with the farm for many years and was considered a "straw boss."[63] She looked like someone who would be called a "straw boss" – she wore a baggie dress over dungarees and wrapped her hair in a bandana. She was a respected community farm leader who was the matriarch of several families who had spent many summers at Capella's. She would come in front of each shack and bang the cowbell until she was sure we were awake. My first thought upon waking each morning was wishing that I was returning to bed that evening. I was exhausted every morning, wondering how I was going to face the day. But after work and after dinner, I didn't go directly to bed. I hung out in the open area at the front of the shacks, listening to music, playing games and talking with other kids.

Capella Farms rented farmland from neighboring farmers to cultivate. Some of the fields were a thirty-minute ride from the shacks; the trip was in an old school bus to the fields. That half-hour gave us an opportunity to wake up before arriving at the fields. A lot of idle gossip and animated conversations among the workers was common. A person with a portable radio would play songs that were popular in the early 1950s. Tennessee Ernie Ford sang "The Tennessee Waltz" – which I remember for no other reason than that it had an easy melody that would remain in my head long after the song had stopped playing.

Work was always difficult, only sometimes more difficult than at other times. We faced the fields each day and the rows of green string

---

63 A "straw boss" is a junior supervisor or an assistant to a foreman. I didn't really know that at the time, I just knew I had to get up when she rang that bell.

beans appeared endless – although many of the fields were 20 acres or less. Families got their assignment of rows of beans to pick first thing in the morning. Many mornings the fields were covered with dew from a change in overnight temperatures; cool evenings brought much moisture by seven o'clock in the morning. Our long trousers – usually blue jeans (which we called dungarees) – became very wet. Men and women, boys and girls – all wore blue jeans or overalls. The older women wore jeans under their house dresses. We attempted to keep ourselves dry with burlap bean sacks that we made into aprons that reached down to our ankles. We took our aprons off when the sun evaporated the moisture.

Overnight, the fields would turn to mud, and the soil would cake to our legs. Then the mud would turn to dust as the sun rose to make the fields really hot. We wore hats and shielded ourselves as best we could from the hot sun. I can still see my mother dragging herself between the rows of beans – caked with mud in the morning and later covered with dust with the heat of the afternoon sun. Young kids picked beans on their knees, not sitting down as my mother and the older folks would.

A pickup truck parked at the end of the rows of beans carried a wooden barrel of cold water in the morning, which became warmer and warmer throughout the day. By the end of the day we might as well have been drinking hot tea (but without the actual tea). No one had any kind of thermos bottle or jug to keep water cold, and ice was nonexistent in the field. There were no small containers of water with ice cubes to take to the field. The ice boxes in our shacks were not freezers. The large block of ice we got to keep our food cold needed to last a week. We would not think of chopping ice from the ice box into small pieces to take to the fields.

Carl Capella, the owner of the farm and the field boss, made all the decisions about what fields would be worked. These decisions were based in part on when the fields were ready to be picked. The first visit to a green bean (string beans) field was called the "first picking." As fieldworkers, we were instructed to pick the mature beans and not pick the small beans, to allow them to grow larger for a later picking. We would often return to the same field three times. At the third picking the beans were fewer, harder to find, and further apart than on the first and second field visits. With fewer beans, we had to work just as hard and earn less money on "third pickings."

Throughout the day I would carry the full burlap sacks of beans to the end of the row. At the end of the day all of the sacks of beans were stacked, side by side, to be weighed by the farm boss who had a scale on a trailer pulled by his pickup truck. As young kid, I wanted to demonstrate my strength by filling the sack to at least a hundred pounds.

As field workers we had few days off. We only had a free day when it rained or when a crop was not ready to be picked. It was quite rare that some crop was not ready to be picked; we didn't have more than two or three days off during the entire summer. When we did get a day off and it wasn't pouring rain, I would venture off the property with other kids to a swimming hole that was about a mile and a half away from the shacks. The swimming hole was called Burdick's: it was an ideal, picturesque pond of water that had a small waterfall about three feet high that tumbled into the pond. It was an aquatic paradise for us kids who had a day free from hard work to go swimming.

Each day, after work and having had dinner, the young people hung out in the open area in front of the shacks; we listened to music, danced, played games and talked to each other. I often listened to the older boys, who were in high school – which I would attend the following academic year, in the fall of 1952. Carl "D" (for Di Pasquale) was one boy's, name; or at least that what was how everybody referred to him. He was the embodiment of a cool stud. He would have been the perfect model for the role of The Fonz on *Happy Days*, the TV sitcom that aired 25 years later. Carl talked, making the case for why Buffalo Technical High School (Tech) was the best public high school in Buffalo. Another Tech student named Bobby, of Spanish heritage (one of the few non-Italians at the farm), was more reserved than Carl D. Bobby also said Tech was the best school in the city.

The two boys obviously made an impression on me as Tech was the only high school I considered attending.

Tech was a central high school, which allowed all qualified boys from the entire city to attend.[64] Prospective students had to take an entrance test and be interviewed by the principal or vice principal. These few standards – taking a written test and being interviewed – are relatively modest by today's academic criteria, but they were sufficient to separate Tech from all the other Buffalo public high schools in the early 1950s.

On some occasions local kids from the Gowanda area worked in the fields alongside us. At the end of the workday the kids from the Gowanda be would be transported back home, not to the shacks. They were day workers. They worked primarily to earn income for their own use, not for family needs. I learned this by overhearing a college girl say that she was earning spending money to return to nearby Cornell University. What was Cornell University? What was the Ivy League? The only Cornell I knew of was an actor named Cornel Wilde. The young girl working the fields was living in a different world than anyone she worked alongside. We did not socialize after work. We went our separate ways and into our separate worlds.

Her world would begin to make sense to me years later, when I was in graduate school earning my doctorate in political science. It would take a few years, but I would come to appreciate how far away her world was from the shacks.

As I reflect on what I write, my description reads as starker and more demanding than what I recall feeling at the time; conditions were acceptable and were "the way things were." I have come to understand and see the value in what may be now described as difficult circumstances. All work for me after I left Gowanda was tolerable in large part because of the experience I gained working on a farm for what I considered a noble cause—to contribute to our family's well-being. Most importantly, I also understood that my farm work was only temporary.

---

64 By today's standards, Tech would be classified as an 'elite' magnet school, although those terms weren't used at that time.

Farm Talk Becomes My Reality

I did attend Tech High School in the fall of 1952. After gaining admission as a student, I came to realize that if I did not keep passing grades, I would be returned to my district high school. Almost half the students who entered Tech were asked to leave or voluntarily transferred to other high schools. I was determined to graduate from Tech.

What I found was that many classmates were very bright and many went on to impressive careers. I also found I was in the middle of the pack again. What surprised me most was that social studies and history were still my academic interests, not mathematics. I had to work hard to grasp that mathematics was necessary for becoming an engineer – and I learned that I definitely wasn't going to be an engineer. The study of history, political science and sociology came to me easily and were interesting subjects. I started to read and pay more attention to the social studies. I concentrated on these subjects throughout high school, although they were not considered to be an integral part of the curriculum.

Gowanda Continues to Have an Impact: A Coincidental Meeting in 1968

Seventeen years after first going to Gowanda to work in 1951, I was an Assistant Professor at the University of Arizona. In the summer of 1968, I received a funding award to attend a political science conference at the University of Michigan in Ann Arbor. It was a chance for me to spend time "back home," since the drive from Buffalo to Ann Arbor was relatively short.

My family – my wife Patti, and our three young daughters (4-year-old Marianne, 2-year-old Shelley, and Melissa, six months old) – and I flew from Tucson, Arizona to Buffalo. We spent the entire summer with my in-laws in North Tonawanda, close to Buffalo where my parents still lived. I borrowed my dad's car to drive to Michigan to attend the conference.

The conference focused on my research interests in state and local government; scholars specializing in state and local policy from around the country attended. At the end of the first day's session, I asked if anyone would be interested in playing handball before dinner. One professor – Brett W. Hawkins from University of Georgia – said that he was interested in playing. We agreed to meet in the parking lot, and from there I would drive us to the University of Michigan Fieldhouse.

We met in the parking lot and walked to my dad's car, which had New York State license plates. The plates signaled that the car was from Erie County – where Buffalo is located. When Brett saw the license, he asked, "Is that an Erie County, New York license plate? Are you from Erie County?" I said it was my dad's car, which I had borrowed to drive to Ann Arbor. I mentioned that I had grown up in Buffalo but had left several years before to attend graduate school.

He said he was from Erie County, also – from a small village named Gowanda. "I'm sure you're not familiar with it." I had to laugh – "Oh yes," I said, "I'm familiar with Gowanda. I worked at Capella's Farm in Gowanda as a kid for three summers. We would go into Gowanda occasionally to Farner & Parker's Ice Cream Parlor."

Brett was surprised that anyone was familiar with Gowanda – and was particularly startled to learn that someone from the University of Arizona had once worked in the Gowanda area. Brett talked about growing up there, and we each shared a few of our memories of the area. As we talked, we realized we had both swam at Burdick's swimming hole. We may have even been there at the same time.

As it turned out, our meeting was quite consequential – even though it was 15 years since I had last worked in Gowanda in 1954. After the conference we stayed in touch. The following year a faculty position became available in the Political Science Department at the University of Georgia. I applied and sent the search committee my vitae and references. I was given an offer to join the faculty at the University of Georgia as an Associate

Professor, which I accepted. I am sure Brett had some influence in my obtaining a faculty position at UGA in 1969.

I knew little about universities when I worked at Capella's as a kid. I didn't have much understanding of the difference between Cornell and Buffalo State; I didn't even know that I would be going on to college. The thought never entered my mind that I would become a university professor when I was working on Capella's farm in Gowanda – yet I went on to a career in higher education. And years later my life – and the lives of my family – would be changed by a chance meeting of two kids who may have been in the same swimming hole on a hot summer day.

The impact of becoming a competitive swimmer and those summers in Gowanda was critical in moving me forward in my life. Mr. Speidel's role in helping me become a competitive swimmer gave me an appreciation of how a great teacher could change a student's life. Swimming itself gave me confidence and a sense of pride not to mention a lifelong relationship with the pool. Gowanda cemented my work ethic and gave me perspective about what hard work really was. These two "extracurricular" activities impacted my approach to school – and so many other aspects of my life, and how I understood the world around me.

CHAPTER 7 :

FINISHING THE FOUNDATION

Buffalo did not have middle schools. Five-year-old kindergarteners and 14-year-old eighth graders all attended school in the same building – along with a few 16-year-olds who had not passed a grade or two. It was truly one school for all. This wide range in age and social development of students presented educational challenges to teachers and students alike. The seventh and eighth grades were separated a bit from the lower grades. Those classrooms were on a separate floor that basically functioned as a middle school. This was the only separation between "middle school" and the earlier grades.

Getting My Bearings as a Student

I was not considered a promising student until the sixth grade. There were several relatively small reasons for my transition from average to someone that several teachers recognized as having academic potential.

In the sixth grade, Mrs. Stroh was a serious, no nonsense teacher. I paid attention, as did all the students. Mrs. Stroh gave the class a weekly geography quiz after we had covered each chapter in the textbook. The quizzes were not major, comprehensive exams – they just covered a single chapter. On one quiz, I answered all ten questions correctly. To my surprise

– as well as Mrs. Stroh's – no one else in the class had answered even seven of the ten questions correctly. I was the only student to "pass" the quiz. The quiz was on the Soviet Union, referred to by most students and me as Russia. In 1950 the United States in a Cold War was locked in a Cold War with the Soviet Union. Mrs. Stroh singled me out and requested that I stand. She cited me as an example of a good student who did his homework. I liked being praised before the class.

What really happened was that I had taken note of some photos in the textbook that showed Russia having oil wells, wheat fields, industrial plants, and factories. At that time, education (and discussion generally) about the Soviet Union focused on it as a country that spread communism throughout the world; it was the enemy of the United States and other democracies. It was backward and evil.

Most of the questions on that quiz were structured in a way that *could* indicate that the Soviet Union was not a powerful modern country – but that was the easy answer, not the right answer. The textbook photos I had taken note of almost seemed to contradict several of the quiz questions. I realized that all the quiz questions about the chapter were framed in a way that could be understood as having the idea that the USSR was weak and lacking in industry and power. But there was more: the questions really made sense only if I answered by acknowledging that Russia was a powerful country having many resources and an industrial base. I suppose most of the other students were expressing what was common thinking at that time – that the Soviet Union was an evil and a backward nation. Most of my classmates felt that Russia was not sufficiently powerful to challenge United States, and that is how they must have answered the questions.

After Mrs. Stroh praised me in front of the entire class as a good student and a role model, I started to take school a little more seriously; receiving personal recognition and praise made a big difference for me. This praise and attention went a long way -- it provided me with the motivation I needed to be a better student.

The seventh and eighth grades were considered the "real" middle school. The seventh and eighth grades had home rooms, where attendance and morning announcements were held before changing classrooms for different teachers and subject teachers (Ms. Williams for English, Ms. Reiman for social studies, etc.). All students, from kindergartners to eighth graders, shared the same cafeteria and playground. The length of the school day was the same for all students, with the exception of the kindergarteners, who were released earlier.

PS52 offered a functional approach to having a middle school and their effort was laudable. They also changed how we as students were organized. The seventh and eighth grades were each stratified into three classes by each student's past performance and teacher expectations of their potential.[65]

I was assigned to the middle of the three seventh grade classes; this is probably about where I belonged. I was an average student, though motivated to do better. I felt satisfied by not being in the lowest seventh grade class. Being near the top of the "middle" (or "average") seventh grade class posed no problem for me. I had been with the same group of students for a couple of years and felt comfortable among them. I performed well in most classes, and was near the top in math, reading and social studies. The exception was spelling – a separate and required subject at the time.[66] English was also a bit of a challenge for me, although my English grades were in the mid-70s.

What was more important to me was that I was not at the bottom of the three classes – among the disinterested and poor performing students who some considered "dummies." I as well as some other students were

---

65 This practice still exists and is called tracking; it was fairly new when I experienced it (schools started doing this in the 1930s). It has been subjected to substantial (and legitimate) criticism since the 1990s, largely because decisions about what "track" students are placed in is generally the result of some combination of standardized testing and teacher input. These measures often reflect racial and gender bias and have historically resulted in many students being misplaced and their full potential not being recognized.
66 The reason for my difficulties with spelling would become clear to me many years later, when it was determined that I have a mild form of dyslexia. This diagnosis was not available in the early 1950s.

aware that the three classes were stratified. Of course, I did not know or use the term stratified at that time. The classes were grouped according to how teachers thought we would perform. I wanted to perform well in class, but not be considered a "smart aleck."

Smart girls were expected to be smart. But I had some concern because high-performing boys – who were considered "smarties" – were subjected to harassment by older kids who did not care much about school. These boys – most of whom had repeated a class or two, and so were older than their classmates – were tougher than the rest of the kids, and they didn't mind demonstrating it.

If someone asked me how I did on a test or exam, my response was usually "OK" – not that I had gotten an A. I did get A's occasionally. Smart boys who did not mask that they had good grades were subjected to ridicule and more.

I was ready to start the eighth grade in September 1951, after having spent the entire summer picking fruit and vegetables in Gowanda. I had matured during those two and a half months. I was now ready to return to school, much more eager than I had been before. I understood, for the first time, how lucky I was to attend school. I did not want to work as a laborer, doing back-breaking work for the rest of my life.[67] I also started to think generally about having a career, with no particular career in mind. I started to think about attending Buffalo Technical High School to become an engineer.

I entered the eighth grade on the day after Labor Day, 1951. I had been assigned to the top of the three 8th grade classes. I was quite surprised and honored to be assigned to the top academic class for my final year at PS52. The recognition of being in the "smart" class was important to

67 My father's formal schooling was halted in the third grade in Italy by my grandfather (for whom I was named, but never met). My father often said, "you don't want to break your back working hard all your life. Go to school, be a good student and get a job where you can dress up with a white shirt and wear a tie to work." My father's motivation was that I get the education that he had been denied. Little did I know that going to work in a white shirt and tie was different than becoming educated. I did go on to college and graduate school which changed my character, not just my clothing. I learned that education was something of a double-edged sword.

my self-image as a student. I had never admitted this to anyone; and most importantly, I had never admitted it to myself until I saw my name on the class list posted on the board by the classroom door. It was only at that moment that I understood for myself the meaning of being placed in that class.

Being placed in a top class made me proud; I had been recognized as a good student, for whatever reason. I tried and succeeded in living up to the "promotion" to the top eighth-grade class, where good grades were acceptable. And there was another benefits as there were no 16-year-old bullies in the top class to see how well I did on an exam or how I behaved in class generally and take me to task for it after school.

I suspect that behavior and deportment had something to do with my being selected to the top of the three classes. My grades were not all that high, but the eighth-grade teachers recognized me as a student with potential. That is how I believe my deportment came in as a factor for my selection. I was not a troublemaker. I was a hard worker and tenacious. I did not give up easily on any assignments. I did my homework and also asked many questions. I think some teachers interpreted my being inquisitive as being bright.

My parents had no awareness that anything had really changed in school; for them, I was just in a class, such as a seventh grade or eighth grade. For my parents, all classes were the same, the only difference among the classes was the teacher.

Eighth grade provided a new educational culture for me. Academic performance and classroom participation were valued by my classmates, as well as by the teachers. Many of the kids in my eighth-grade class were academic achievers in comparison to the kids in the other classes. But this is relative. I am not certain as I look back now how well I would have competed academically with some of the students in Buffalo's affluent suburban eighth-grade classes.

Most of the students in my class were courteous (or at least not mean) to one another, and attentive to the teachers. Student behavior was more like that which I suspect was to be found in suburban schools. Years later, I came to better understand the expectations of middle-class families for their children's success.

In the eighth grade I had several excellent teachers for several subjects. I suspect that their teaching, like our behavior, was more akin to what was found in suburban schools, and they felt they were making good use of their time instructing us. But there was one class, and one teacher, that especially made an impression on me.

In the eighth grade, Ms. Ruth Reiman was my American history teacher. She had a reputation for knowing her stuff and being a tough teacher and a disciplinarian. Students did not fool around in her class and certainly did not mess with her. She took no guff from boys who towered over her. She was 4 feet and 10 inches tall, while several of the boys were "six footers". It did not take much for her to keep the class in line.

She knew social studies and was able to teach from the textbook – and more. She engaged students in acting out historical issues and events from the textbook. She involved students in classroom activities where we took on the roles of the historical characters and issues we studied. This acting out of historical issues in class was quite an innovative approach to teaching in the early 1950s. (Of course, we had to read the textbook before participating in a historical acting performance.)

In our American History textbook, there was a unit on the Labor Movement in the United States. Ms. Reiman assigned students who had read the assignments to play the roles of management and labor during a contract negotiation. This was an activity built around the shop union representative in a furniture manufacturing factory, who was threatening management with a strike.

I was assigned the role of a labor union representative who had to negotiate with management concerning a salary increase, more benefits and better working conditions for workers. The student playing the manager resisted my attempts at persuasion to raise worker's salaries. We argued back and forth for a while about the amount of a pay increase and the need for an increase in benefits, such as workplace safety and two fifteen-minute work breaks in an eight-hour work shift. There was no budging by either the student in the role of plant manager or me as the union representative. In an off the cuff comment, I said, "Well, if you don't want to give the workers a pay raise, we won't make any tables and chairs. All your customers won't have tables and chairs, because we won't make any. They can sit on the floor for dinner with no chairs and tables."

Ms. Reiman really thought that was funny and reflective of the unit on labor-management relationships. She congratulated me in front of the class for understanding the topic and "bringing energy" to the classroom. From then on, she always looked upon me fondly as adding passion to scholarship. Recognition by teachers, especially Ms. Reiman, was an important stimulus to my academic motivation.

Extracurricular Activities

I participated in a few extracurricular activities in eighth grade, in addition to being a member of the swim team.

School Newspaper Reporter

I wrote a couple articles for the school newspaper. To be clear, the school newspaper was mimeographed[68] on legal-sized paper, no more than eight pages in length, typed double-spaced on one side. An article for our school paper was a single paragraph – on rare occasion two or three paragraphs. I wrote an article about our principal, Principal Ford R. Park. I found it interesting that he had two last names-- Ford and Park.

My article was about Mr. Park's days at Syracuse University, when he was captain of the football team in 1910 and 1911. I came to write the story when I saw Mr. Park running in the playground to help someone who had

---

68 Mimeograph machines were a precursor to the modern photocopy machine.

fallen down. Mr. Park was in his 60s in 1952. He was surprisingly fast for a man of his age. I approached Mr. Park when I saw that, and I told him that I was surprised by how fast he ran.

He said that as a young man he was captain of the Syracuse University football team. He went on to tell me that his most memorable experience on the football team was tackling Jim Thorpe, All-American, Olympian and considered by many the best athlete of the 20th century. I found it interesting that Mr. Ford remembered a single football tackle as the highlight of his football career at Syracuse.

After the school newspaper was distributed, I was called to the principal's office. Mr. Park congratulated me on writing a piece on his football career. He remarked that I was a good researcher to have dug up information about him that occurred so many years before. I did not have the heart to tell him that he had told me the story a few days earlier. Mr. Park's memory was fading, which I now better understand, as I am now two decades older than he was at that time.[69]

School Safety Patrol

During the eighth grade I was also a member of the school safety patrol. As a member of the safety patrol I got to wear a shiny badge on a white belt across my chest. The duty of the safety patrol member was to guide younger students across the street. There were police officers who escorted kids across the major intersection at Grant and Forest; we were stationed at the smaller intersections. There were no painted crosswalks at which students should cross the street.

One day, during lunch period, an armored truck parked next to my safety patrol station. The driver and the armed guard got out and crossed the street to buy donuts at a bakery. Before they returned, I noticed that they had left the keys in the back door of the armored truck. The vehicle

---

69 Ford Park was actually captain of the Syracuse football team in 1907 (https://en.wikipedia.org/wiki/1907_Syracuse_Orangemen_football_team). Syracuse played the Carlisle Indian Industrial School every year in the early 20th century; it is likely that Mr. Park tackled Jim Thorpe during Thorpe's first year on the team (https://sports.jrank.org/pages/4841/Thorpe-Jim-Chronology.html).

could have been entered and any money they had been delivering or collecting could have been taken. I took the keys out and returned them to the driver when he returned. The two men looked terrified that the contents of the armored truck could have been stolen. They were clearly concerned that the mistake might be discovered by their supervisor who might reprimand them or fire them. I was not thanked for returning the keys as I expected; no recognition at all was offered to me. They left quickly. What was I thinking?

The Ugly Underbelly of School

There were a number of kids, mostly boys, that were 16 years old and in the eighth grade; a couple of these "big" kids drove cars. I remember an incident where George Pollar – the toughest kid at PS52 – had gotten himself a girlfriend to go along with his car. One afternoon, George backed his car up along the curb with the rear door open – pinning Teddy Kaminski (a mild-mannered, nerdy kid) to a telephone pole. George inched the car back, squeezing Teddy between the door and the pole. Teddy was not injured but could not escape the pressure of the car door pressing him against the telephone poll. I am sure he was scared and humiliated.

There were several guys and a few girls who witnessed this incident. It was over in a few minutes, but no one missed the message of who was boss. I was there. I said nothing. No one – including me – offered Teddy any protection or came to his aid. I was just glad that I was not the object of the humiliating event.

Bullying came often, and in many forms. There were other, even more humiliating bullying incidents throughout the 8th grade. Some cases, although not identified as "bullying" at the time, I am certain left life-long emotional scars on their victims.

A New Uncle

On May 10, 1952, near the end of the eighth-grade school year, I gained an uncle; Frank Doerfler married my Aunt Rose Gardo.[70] I gained a quirky uncle who changed my life.[71]

Frank and Rose had dated for several years. I appreciated and liked Frank and had hoped they would marry, but I was not sure they would. Frank was not Italian, and Rose was very picky in everything she did, including what she thought of men. I had even heard adults question whether Aunt Rose would ever marry.

Aunt Rose and Uncle Frank on their wedding day, 1952.

---

70 Rose was the aunt who responded to Gertrude with my grandmother during the 1940 census.
71 http://www.archives.com/1940-census/frank-doerfler-ny-61034129.

The marriage of Frank E. Doerfler to my Aunt Rose brought a different way of thinking and enjoyment into my life. I affectionately referred to my Uncle as "Franchie Doorker." It was an endearing name that he, did in fact, appreciate as a complement.

Rose and Frank were quite different in character. Aunt Rose was cold, stern and difficult to approach, particularly for children. In contrast Uncle Frank was open, warm, approachable, and often quirky. Some in my Gardo family did not know what to make of him. He was even sometimes a bit childish – at least that was what the adults thought, particularly the men. I disagreed with those who thought he was childish – he was more a child at heart. I saw value in his ability to communicate with young kids, especially me. I was in the eighth grade when they married; and their wedding was an important event in my life. His membership into the Gardo family was a "breath of fresh air" for me and some of the other Gardo grandchildren.

Upon first meeting Uncle Frank, one could not help but notice that his eyes were not coordinated and did not jointly focus on anything he looked at. He wasn't cross-eyed, but his eyes focused in different directions at the same time, much like antiaircraft searchlights examining the night sky for enemy aircraft. His eyes individually rotated in different directions, as if on a quest to make sure that the enemy was spotted as they approached; I had seen this on weekly newsreels and in movies about WWII. When talking to Frank one-on-one I noticed that his eyes seemed to be on objects that were beyond me. As Frank became tired toward the end of the day or when I assisted him in the morning on his milk route, his eyes would begin to move independently of each other.

I learned that Frank's eyes were damaged during combat in World War II. Frank was not quite 20 years old when he enlisted in the U.S. Navy. His ship was bombed while on a mission planned in the Mediterranean in coordination with the D Day invasion at Normandy (Overlord); Frank's ship was part of Operation Dragoon.[72] I recall him mentioning that as German Luftwaffe was strafing his ship and he was climbing down the ladder to the lower deck, he stepped on a sailor who had been shot and lay dead at the bottom of the steps. He said it was the worst feelings he ever had as he felt his foot sink into the sailor's back.His eyes were damaged by a German Luftwaffe bomb that exploded on his ship's deck, but I never knew any details about his injury. He never talked much about it, and no one questioned him about his war experience, this just was not discussed during that era. It had to have been a war injury as he could not have possibly passed the physical for military service with such poor eye coordination.

But it seems he was not recognized for this service injury by family members. In 1990, when he died, there was no Purple Heart Medal to be found among his belongings. He must have been awarded the Purple Heart, yet it was never a topic of conversation within our family. No one ever thought that he had been awarded a medal. There was never any discussion of his injury, hospital stay or recovery.[73]

Frank grew up and spent his childhood during the Great Depression and soon after he completed high school, the United States entered World War II. The Great Depression left its mark on him even though he was from a middle-class family. His father worked as skilled tool and die maker. As an only child, I imagine that Frank suffered only moderate economic hardship compared to many other Buffalo youngsters, but the harsh economic conditions affected the entire population in some way. Few persons escaped the impact of the Great Depression except the very rich, and not all of them escaped the negative economic effects, either.

---

72 This was a large and important mission that is not well-known in contemporary culture. Operation Dragoon, originally planned to be coordinated with D Day, began on August 15, 1944. A brief introduction can be found at https://en.wikipedia.org/wiki/Operation_Dragoon.
73 This is all very strange, because Frank clearly met the criteria to be awarded the Purple Heart: "The Purple Heart Medal is awarded to members of the armed forces of the U.S. who are wounded by an instrument of war in the hands of the enemy and posthumously to the next of kin in the name of those who are killed in action or die of wounds received in action. It is specifically a combat decoration." (PurpleHeart.org). There is no comprehensive list of Purple Heart recipients; Frank's name is not found on any of the partial lists that are on the Internet.

Aunt Rose and Uncle Frank did not have children. My brothers, sisters and I were their surrogate children. Uncle Frank was a breath of fresh air because he was the first adult family member who treated kids as kids – with joy. He enjoyed being with me, my brothers and cousins while we were still kids and acted as kids usually do. He would take me and my brothers, Benny and Joey, and neighborhood kids swimming at Crystal Beach and Sherkston Quarry few miles beyond the Peace Bridge in Canada. He owned a car when I was not old enough to even get a learner's permit. We would spend the entire day swimming during the summer. He was the only relative that not only took us swimming – but swam with us. He enjoyed being in the water with us kids. Providing transportation for swimming and being with kids gave him a great deal of pleasure.

Our trips to Canada to swim were always a bit unusual. There was an admission fee for each person entering Sherkston Quarry. At Frank's suggestion, some of us kids would hide in the trunk of the car in order to avoid paying the entrance fee. When we got to the admission gate at Sherkston we paid for those sitting in the car's cabin. One boy and occasionally two boys riding in the car's trunk went undetected and did not pay admission.

When we went swimming at Crystal Beach kids didn't have to ride in the trunk – there was no admission fee at Crystal Beach Amusement Park. But there was a fence around the entrance to the swimming area which we had to crawl under to enter the beach to avoid the admission fee to the beach to swim.

I recall that once we got to Crystal Beach we would have to change quickly into our swimsuits and crawl under the fence before we were detected. Frank taught me a lesson concerning my usual method of dressing and undressing. As I was undressing to put on my swimsuit, I started to take off my shirt first and then I was going to take off my pants and put on my swimsuit. Uncle Frank advised me to take off my pants first, put on my swim trunks and then worry about the shirt later. His logic of dressing quickly and in a prescribed order, so as not to get caught by Crystal Beach Park attendants, would never have occurred to me.

Each time we went swimming Frank told many stories of "Stanley Duck." Stanley Duck was a mythical fictitious figure that Frank created. Stanley was a great swimmer who went to Kensington High School with Frank. According to Uncle Frank, I should live up to Stanley Duck's swimming accomplishments. He encouraged me to swim.

After the War, Uncle Frank worked as a milk man for Jones Dairy in Buffalo. In the early 1950's, milk was delivered in glass bottles by truck directly to homes on a prescribed route. On many occasions, particularly on holidays, I would help him deliver the milk. I always helped on New Year's morning, when Frank would be tired from staying out late celebrating on New Year's Eve. He needed and appreciated my assistance.

I often went with him on his route; sometimes we went to the suburb of Tonawanda, other times we went to the African American section of Buffalo. These areas were quite different from my own, and I had been unaware that such difference in neighborhoods existed. We would discuss the two areas and who lived there and what the people were like. One area was a white working-class suburb, newly built after World War II. The other route covered a large segment of African American segregated public housing on the near Eastside of Buffalo. These were a very different worlds from where I lived. I had no conception of suburbs, never having knowingly visited one before delivering milk with Uncle Frank. We had had public housing near my Busti Avenue neighborhood, but those residents were exclusively white.

I also had as much free chocolate milk as I wanted when assisting my Uncle Frank. He would say, "Vinny, drink from that quart bottle of chocolate milk. You will really like it." I asked him if I had to pay for the chocolate milk I drank. His answer was no. He would say, "All I have to do is break the glass bottle when you're finished. I don't get charged for broken milk bottles." He said I could have more if I wanted. Uncle Frank was not above skirting the law with petty larceny. Free chocolate milk was one of the perks of being a milkman's helper.

Uncle Frank owned a 1951 Ford Fairlane – a beautiful car which he kept in immaculate condition. He did this, in part, by asking me to assist him in the washing and polishing of the car. We used Simonize auto wax, and Frank guided me to make sure that we covered every square inch of the car so that it sparkled. I polished the car one section at a time while he stood at a distance, making certain that I covered all areas and left no streaks. He was fastidious about how the car was washed and polished. Although we didn't use spit, he said it was a "spit shine." I worked hard to meet his expectations and was rewarded with an evening dinner.

After washing and polishing the car I was always a dinner guest at my Aunt Rose and Uncle Frank's house. I enjoyed those dinners. They ate dinner with place settings, including the appropriate silverware. I was treated as their guest. I did not have to share their attention or the dinner table with my brothers and sisters. I paid attention to my manners when I was a guest at their house as I feared my Aunt Rose would not soon invite me again. But that never happened – I was always welcomed.

Uncle Frank had graduated from Buffalo's Kensington's High School. After his military service, he did not take advantage of the G.I. Bill of Rights and to continue his education. When he came home from his military service he worked for Jones Dairy and remained a "blue-collar" working man. He had a series of other blue-collar jobs throughout his life. He never pursed a college education or a skilled trade. Even so, he was quite interested in seeing me get an education. He was quite pleased that I decided to go to the academic Buffalo Technical High School, which was considered the best in the city.

As I entered high school later in the fall of 1952, he gave me a copy of Ernest Hemingway's recently published novel, *The Old Man and the Sea*. He said it was a good book that I should read. Frank also said that Hemingway was America's best author. I do not believe Uncle Frank ever read the book, but he wanted to make sure that I did. I read it as a 14-year-old and I didn't understand that it was an allegory as well as a story of a man and a fish.

Uncle Frank was a curious person and we had many conversations about a variety of subjects. Often, discussions were about commonplace matters, but they always led to questions and new information, insights and things I never thought about. One winter, he had started his car for us to go somewhere, and of course it was cold inside the car given Buffalo's winters, so he turned on the heater. I waited a few seconds and cold air kept coming out of the heater. I asked him why there was no heat. He asked me, "How do you think my car gets heat, Vinnie?" He said, "It takes a while for the car to generate heat. There is a radiator, and the engine has to heat the water in the radiator to generate hot air." I had never given any thought to how a car heater worked and generated heat. Frank took the time to explain relatively simple things in a manner that would make sense to a kid. Although what we talked about was often common, the subjects were usually foreign to me. I was ignorant of the many aspects of life that I had not yet encountered. His open and generous explanations provided insight without making me feel uneducated, or worse – stupid.

In addition to discussing how things worked, we also had more academic discussions. We talked about the cause and purpose of war. Uncle Frank thought that all wars were fought for the purpose of reducing population. That seemed like strange reasoning from someone who fought the Nazis in World War II. As I look back, I don't think he believed that theory, but wanted to have a discussion about war that would raise all sorts of questions and possible responses. He encouraged me to think rationally and present my case in a logical manner. Many of these discussions were in his car or in the milk truck when I was helping him make his deliveries.

Even popular music was a source of discussion. Frank was fond of songs that were popular a decade or more before he came into my life. He sang songs that were popular during the Great Depression such as "Life is Just a Bowl of Cherries," and "The Music Goes Round and Round and Comes Out Here." These popular tunes depicted his youth amid the uncertain, challenging economic conditions of the Great Depression. We discussed that money was not everything, and that life had other values as well. While I understood that life is more than a bowl of cherries, I found it hard to believe that the "music goes round and round" meant anything in particular. The two songs had catchy melodies that I liked. Later I came to realize these songs reflected an optimistic attitude toward confronting the economic hardships of the Great Depression.

Frank introduced topics in conversations that would never have occurred to me or would have been raised by my parents or other relatives. For example, he said he was not afraid of dying, but he was afraid of a painful death. At that age I was a devout Roman Catholic who had been taught that there was life after death; that after death a person would either go to heaven or hell, depending on how the person led his life. As for young children who did not have an opportunity to have much of a life or have any sins, there would be a place called limbo, in between heaven and hell, where a child would put in some time before going to heaven. If a person was a little older and had not committed any mortal sins (as opposed to venial sins), that person would go to purgatory until the sins were washed away before entering heaven. Before listening to Uncle Frank, I held the belief that death meant the possibility of going to Hell—*forever and ever.*

I don't think that my father or my biological uncles believed in heaven and hell after death. We never discussed religion and the afterlife. Religion was not a topic of conversation between my family's male adults and children. Adult Italian men had a different view of religion than did the women. Few men in my family went to church on Sunday. None of my relatives ever thought about becoming a priest as it was not considered a real career choice. I found out as I grew older that many Italian men had an anti-cleric sentiment. They felt that priests took advantage of the women's attachment to the Church.[74]

If Frank wasn't a Catholic, my aunt wouldn't have married him. He was of German heritage and had a more rational view of religion than the men in my family. He had different opinions about religion and many other subjects. He was not a nonbeliever, but held a different, less doctrinaire, and less literal understanding of Catholic Scripture. Generally, Uncle Frank brought to my family a perspective on many subjects that were different than I was previously exposed to and did not question before meeting him.

As I look back, it didn't matter to me whether my Uncle Frank was correct or accurate about any of the topics we discussed. He was thought-provoking, and when I challenged him, there was much he said with which I disagreed. I learned a lot from an "in-law relative" who cared about me making something of myself.

Frank got me thinking.

Eighth Grade: A Postscript

After I graduated from elementary school, my father started working at PS52; his official job title was fireman. He was referred to as custodian by the teachers and a janitor by students. His job was to attend to the coal furnace. During the long cold winter in Buffalo he was there every day, for most of the day. My father's "office" next to the boiler consisted of a chair and a desk that held the work orders of the day.

During that era, many teachers at PS52 smoked, including Ms. Reiman. My father also smoked; Chesterfields was his brand of cigarettes. The faculty that smoked cigarettes went down to the school boiler room in the basement during their free periods, and especially during their lunch

---

74 As my grandfather grew older he was more inclined to go to church on Sundays; he became an usher and collected donations during services.

hour. My father smoked and talked with teachers who visited the boiler room daily.

This practice continued on for many years after I had graduated from PS52. Years later, the teachers would still talk with my father while they smoked; by that time, I had graduated from Michigan State University, having earned a Ph.D. My name would still come up in their discussions. My father was obviously proud that I had become a university professor. He would have liked to become a teacher if his father had not taken him out of school to tend goats.

No less proud was Ms. Reiman. I may have been her only student, or one of very few, to choose an academic career in the social sciences. I think she might have said, "If Vinny can do it, it was possible for any student to succeed in education." Of course, that could only happen if they paid attention in her class and worked hard.

Eight years after I graduated, my sisters Angie and Kathy also were students in Ms. Reiman's class. They indicated that Ms. Reiman would remark to the class about what I had said in her class eight years before. Ms. Reiman said that taking her class had helped me go on to become a scholar. She would say that the janitor's son really went far in social studies and that she had contributed to my success. It was true, she did contribute to my becoming a university professor. Without her, I may not have gotten the recognition and encouragement I needed to pursue a career in higher education.

Ms. Reiman never married, and she had no children of her own. She looked upon some of her students as if they were her nephews and nieces, if not her children.[75] Education was Ms. Reiman's profession, passion, and contribution to the lives of working-class kids. She was a compassionate and dedicated teacher who left a mark on many students — and certainly on me. (See Appendix C for how I utilized Ms. Reiman's encouragement

---

75 She did not view all of her students this way; several PS52 students, including a few of my classmates, were convicted of serious crimes and served prison sentences.

while pursuing my education at Michigan State University in political science.)

From polio to Ms. Reiman, these were the years that built the foundation for all that would come – not just for me personally, but for the United States as a nation. As I look over the landscape of my life, I see how the personal, economic, and social currents that I saw and felt during these years have manifested as changes, and failures to change, in our country. From the 1940 census to the 2020 census – and from polio to our current Covid 19 pandemic – then and now.

EPILOGUE:

BACK AND FORTH ACROSS DECADES

In 2020 there were far fewer Gertrude K. Bunces, Census Enumerators. The census was largely distributed and collected by the US Post Office and over the internet. Initially there was no army of enumerators – of any name – blanketing the country to conduct census interviews in 2020; COVID-19 made in-person contact dangerous. Personal contact with households was selective and primarily used as a follow-up to survey hard-to-reach people, fill in gaps in information, and for quality control. Statistical methods utilizing big data were relied upon to assure accurate and valid counts of persons and responses. Although 1940 was the first census to employ statistical methods in the collection of data, it looks like the statistical dark ages when compared to 2020.

Sorry, Gertrude – you have been largely replaced.

In his celebrated novel *The Go-Between* (1953), L. P. Hartley wrote, "The past is a foreign country, they do things differently there." [76] The truth of this has continued to be brought home to me as I have detailed my childhood in the "extended" 1940s (1938-1952). It has been a challenge for me to sort out this time, let alone explain what growing up in this era meant in

---

76 Hartley's work has been adapted for the screen several times; the 1971 screenplay was authored by Harold Pinter and won the *Palme d'Or* at the 1971 Cannes Film Festival. More recently, the book was adapted for television in 2015 by the BBC.

terms that would make sense to today's young people (and interested readers generally). I have truly wrestled with what I remembered of that past, careful to assess my thinking at that time with an eye toward how it might be understood by readers using today's standards.

History never repeats itself. History only rhymes.

—Mark Twain

Reading the 1940 census provoked my interest to reflect on the past, actually my past, eight decades ago. With respect to Mark Twain's quote I believe that history is only one way to probe the past. Obviously, memoirs are based on memory to tap the past; and memories in turn are invoked by persons and events that had special and lasting meaning to me. I was aware that I was probing my past from the way I think today. I was especially careful not to be captured by nostalgia, or exhibit overt bias in telling my story, as I currently recall it. That is why I refer to what I have written as "musings" on my early youth. After all, I constructed conversations, created scenes and described events at which I was not present. The past was certainly different from the present. Yet, studying the past provided me with a perspective for better understanding the present.

Polio-Covid 19

I offer a few closing reflections of my experiences with polio with the Covid-19. The two viruses are not the same, yet rhyme. In contrasting them, as I observed and experienced them, it has provided me with perspective on Covid-19 and other potential viruses that are yet to arrive.

In late 2019, a few news outlets began reporting about a mysterious respiratory flu that was sweeping across China, centered in a city most Americans had never heard of called Wuhan. But this wasn't really "just a flu" – it was killing people. And then in early 2020, it became clear that whatever this was, it was no longer just in China. Europeans began to get sick, and then the disease showed up in the United States. Suddenly this

21st century world did not feel so very different from the world when I contracted polio in 1939.

COVID-19 now, polio then, spawned public fear in my early and my later years. The two viruses were not the same disease, their structure differed, how they were transmitted differed, how they were treated differed. The polio virus was ingested through mouth into the digestive system effecting the nervous system. Covid-19 was primarily spread by inhaling virus droplets in the air through the lungs while breathing. Many persons contracting each virus were asymptomatic but were nevertheless able to transmit the virus to others. The two diseases did share a similar single characteristic: both generated public fear.

Quarantine and isolation of polio victims was mirrored by CDC recommendations for the need of those infected to be quarantined. Effective means to prevent and limit the spread of COVID-19 was for persons to separate themselves by six feet, referred to as "social distancing," and wearing masks was required.

Given polio's long period of uncertainty regarding how it was transmitted, government and health officials limited social contacts by closing schools. swimming pools and other venues of social gatherings. No masks were required. Citizens overwhelmingly followed governmental orders in dealing with polio – but much less so with Covid-19.

Indeed, as I was preparing this for publication, Dr, Anthony Fauci made a very similar point. Asked by CNN's Jim Acosta about the misinformation spread by Fox News regarding Covid 19 vaccines, Fauci said," we probably would have polio in this country if we had this kind of false information that's being spread now." He added, "If we had that back decades ago. I would be certain that we'd still have polio in this country."[77]

Central to combating both viruses have been the need for a preventative vaccine. It took several decades to develop a polio vaccine. A vaccine for Covid-19 was created in one year after the virus was identified. It took

---

77 CNN, Ben Tinker and Alla Elassar July 17, 2021.

polio more than a half a century to reach the number of deaths caused by Covid-19 in little more than a year in the U.S. As I write this in June 2021, the number of Covid-19 related deaths has passed six hundred thousand; U.S. Patient #1 was first detected in January 2020.

Medical science has advanced dramatically since 1939. Polio caused paralysis and crippled many persons, mostly children. The display of newspaper photos and motion pictures of crippled and paralyzed children mobilized the public into unified action to conquer polio – which took decades to eliminate. Visuals such as photos and movies, plus the fact that children were the primary victims of polio unified a prolonged nation-wide approach to prevent the disease. I can only imagine how different my childhood and the United States as a whole would have been if a vaccine for polio had been found in just one year.

Polio did not have an impact on the economy. The negative impact of polio was primarily on the victims and their families – not on the economy. Covid-19 has had a dramatic impact on the economy, both in the U.S. and throughout the world. Complicating the comparison between the two viruses were political differences as to how to keep the economy from going into recession, how to keep businesses open and reduce high unemployment levels, all the while containing the transmission of Covid-19.

The international scope of the diseases varied as well. Polio was an epidemic, conquered at first in the United States with little attention to the international pandemic. In 1939, world-wide travel was quite limited in comparison with current global travel.

One virus (polio) was an epidemic treated almost exclusively in the United States. Covid-19 is a pandemic to be attacked world-wide along with conquering the virus in the United States.

Yes, Mr. Twain, history does rhyme. We can, gain perspective on the present by studying the past. With respect to Covid-19 there will be a *next* pandemic. There is no reason to be unprepared: the past has informed us.

We can say that science has changed everything since 1939 – but it is not just the science. It is our willingness to change the social norms, to adapt what science makes possible to how we relate to each other. It becomes necessary to understand that change is really a reflection not just of science, and but of cultural norms that affect behavior – and that these norms have changed substantially over the 80 years since the 1940 census. In 2021, the science is infinitely better, the norms and trust in our leaders and institutions-- less so.

Still Here, Still There

As I muse about the past I keep coming back to Hartley's idea – "The past is a foreign country, they do things differently there"– as this certainly applies to what I have written, what you have read. Although the span of 80 years might not be "the past" to an ancient historian, it seems like an eon from the perspective of where I was then and where I am now. That past has been difficult for me to sort out, difficult to explain, and yet I am the one who lived it. As I have written these words, I have wrestled with what I remembered of the past, careful to assess my thinking and how I express myself, evaluating my words in terms of what I understand of how today's youth could comprehend what I conveyed.

I propose this modification to Hartley's quote: "The present as well as the past are foreign countries which speak differently to me – both then and now." Cultural and social norms in this 21st century are quite different than what I experienced as a child; the life choices available to today's young bear little resemblance to those I had when I was their age. The cultural environment has changed over 80 years. Today's youth are exposed to an expanding universe that includes more diversity and choices and ways of working and living than I would have ever imagined. And their exposure to this expanding world occurs multiple times faster than mine did – or could have.

Of course, I see this continuum because I am both *there* – in the past – and *here* today. Over the course of my lifetime, I have entered several metaphorical foreign cultures – while not leaving the United States. Not only do persons from the past speak a foreign language, I find that in the present persons speak foreign languages – both literally and metaphorically. Conversations take place that are foreign to me -- conversations about iPads and tweets and social networks.

Facts are more easily gathered today, yet the context in which facts are interpreted seems to elude many, or are just not considered at all. A context for grasping the benefits of science should include an understanding of the past. I have found that how we think about the past may also represent the fears and opportunities that are embedded in particular experiences. Polio no longer exists – but the fear around the disease was real. My experience of polio was shrouded in misunderstanding, prejudice and guilt. These conditions were due in part to ignorance and prejudice among public officials, medical professionals and the public.

How will persons in the future understand Covid-19? How will they think about its causes, its spread and how it was dealt with in the United States? What lessons have we learned to prepare us for conquering the next pandemic?

The era and the life about which I have written is the past and covers a period of 14 years during which I also changed considerably. I gave meaning to this time from my *current* thinking, no matter how much I tried to depict who I was or what was occurring at that time. I have related a story of events that took place long ago, relying on evidence that I am perusing *now* – in my contemporary context. The past can only come to life through what we understand in the present. As our understanding of "now" changes, so does our understanding of "then." We need an understanding of the past to better understand the present; and an understanding of the present to better understand the past.

As the 2020 U.S. Census was taken 80 years after Gertrude Bunce walked down Busti Avenue with her clipboard, I live in a very different country. The past is gone, yet its influence remains – upon me and upon my country.

APPENDIX A:

THE LIFE AND TIMES OF GERTRUDE BUNCE

(by Mary Beth Melchior, Ph.D.)

While confirming the date Vince had originally found for Gertrude Bunce's death in 1972, I came up on an obituary for a woman named Kathryn Crowe, who had passed on in Buffalo in 2009. Ms. Crowe was described in the obituary as the daughter of Gertrude Bunce, and she was survived by four nieces and nephews, who were the children of her sister, Mary (Bunce) Swan. As I sketched out the family tree, it became clear that Gertrude had at least four grandchildren: had they even known their grandmother? Could I find them – and would they be willing to talk about any memories of their grandmother they had, or anything they had ever heard about her?

A little bit of research led to the family: Gertrude's middle daughter, Mary, had moved across the Great Lakes to Michigan after she met a dapper young Brit who had just begun a career as an executive with Chrysler. She and her husband had created a family of two boys and two girls in the Oakland County suburbs of Detroit in the late 1950s and early 1960s. All four of these children (now successful adults) were still alive, and though they were children and young teens when their grandmother passed, they remembered her fondly.

Gertrude Bunce was born Gertrude Flynn in Buffalo on December 24, 1891. She came into the world as a breach baby, born to two Irish immigrants. Not much is known about her early life or education, but grandson Greg told us that she was a woman with strong values and boundaries: she found a dining set she wanted for her own home and family and saved her money for nine years until she could purchase that dining set – and only after that, did she get married.

Gertrude Bunce (nee Flynn), circa 1910. Photo courtesy of David Swan.

Gertrude married a Buffalo police officer named Jack Bunce and the couple had three girls before and during the Depression – Kathryn, Mary and Lillian. She raised her three girls to value education: all three went to D'Youville College in Buffalo, a private Catholic college which was (at the time Gertrude's daughters attended) an all-women's school that had been the first in western New York to offer bachelor's degrees to women. Each of Gertrude's three daughters went on to be educators themselves; all went on to earn master's degrees in education.

I was, of course, particularly interested in what her grandchildren might know about Gertrude's work life, and particularly about her work as a Census Enumerator. Her grandsons told us that even throughout the Depression there was always a slow drip of money because of their grandfather's continued employment with the Buffalo police force, but that Gertrude also brought in money to keep the family afloat. She worked a variety of jobs and even had a real estate license. The grandchildren that we spoke with had not known that she had been a Census Enumerator, but they were not surprised: they knew that Gertrude had also been an operator for the telephone company from 1910-1919, and that she had been involved with "the flu survey" at some point in her life.

Jack and Gertrude Bunce, circa late 1940s, in front of their home on Eaglewood Avenue on Buffalo's South Side. Photo Courtesy of David Swan.

Her grandchildren did say that she didn't really drive – her oldest grandson, David, said that he only saw her a drive a couple of times, and that it's likely that she took the bus from her home on Eaglewood Avenue in the Irish neighborhood of South Buffalo to Busti Avenue on Buffalo's West Side – about 7 miles away.[78] That seven miles was, of course, the distance between two different worlds: one very Irish, and one very Italian.

---

78 Gertrude's grandson David does remember his grandfather and grandmother having a Buick "4 holer" – a feature of top-of-the-line Buick models in the 1950s and 1960s. His grandparents often drove across Canada to visit their grandchildren in Michigan.

We asked if they thought Gertrude might have been fearful in coming to Busti Avenue – as Vince states, this was viewed as a "dangerous" neighborhood at that time by many who didn't live there, and Gertrude was a 48-year-old woman coming to this neighborhood alone. Grandson Greg suggested that she probably wasn't afraid because she was so driven by her Catholic faith. He told us that Gertrude was a "righteous" woman, a woman like Mother Theresa of Calcutta – she was not afraid of those who had been stigmatized by society. Had they been able to have a less structured conversation, Gertrude and Nonna Gardo might have found common ground in their commitment to the Catholic Church (though of course they would have needed Aunt Rose to continue translating the conversation).

Gertrude's grandchildren shared many wonderful memories of their grandmother, though of course they didn't come to know her until long after the 1940 Census. They spoke of a woman who always had dinner on the table at 6 p.m., ready to feed her policeman husband as he came home from his beat and put his service revolver in the drawer. They had rib roast every Sunday, and Gertrude loved the Ed Sullivan show. She hummed all the time (in a lilting high voice). She was thrilled by the Apollo 11 moon landing in 1969: a woman who had been born in a time of no cars, no electricity, and no indoor plumbing had lived to see a man walk on the moon. Granddaughter Kathleen remembered her as a "loving grandmother with blue-gray hair and soft powdered skin who smelled like Noxzema and Beechnut gum." Their memories are rich in every way.

Gertrude loved to talk – family breakfasts would often stretch into lunch as the conversation went on. And Gertrude was very much the matriarch of her family: when her daughter Mary had oldest grandson David at Mercy Hospital in Buffalo (just blocks away from Gertrude's home), Gertrude instructed her eldest daughter Kathryn to help with the new baby. Her daughters were grown, but Gertrude was still calling the shots.

Grandson Greg told the family lore of his grandfather's death in 1970: "he came home from work [as a police officer], said he had walked his last beat, and when he went to bed that night he didn't wake up." Gertrude found her husband dead in bed the next morning. She never fully recovered from the loss and died just a couple of years later. She left her three daughters, their husbands, and four grandchildren behind.

Her legacy should not be underestimated: grandson David, a prominent dentist in the Traverse City area of northern Michigan, credits his dental career to a suggestion Gertrude made when he was in junior high school. Grandson Greg joyfully remembers her giving them a "golden Christmas" – giving gifts like a gold Stingray bike and a golden teddy bear. She was the spiritual center of the family for him. Her youngest grandchild, daughter Joanne, was thrilled that we found Gertrude and were recognizing her "unassuming" grandmother as a catalyst for this book.

Gertrude lived a full life that began and ended in the Irish enclave of South Buffalo. I'm so grateful that she had a detour that brought her to Busti Ave. on that precipitous day in 1940 when baby Vince Marando wasn't home – and let me meet her grandchildren in the 21st century.

APPENDIX B:

LETTER TO TIM RUSSERT ON THE PUBLICATION OF
BIG RUSS & ME

In 2004, journalist Tim Russert wrote *Big Russ and Me*, a memoir describing the relationship he had with his father while he was growing up in Buffalo. I was touched by this book – though I recognized that Russert grew up in a very different Buffalo than I had, partly because of place (Russert was from Irish South Buffalo), and partly because of time (Russert was about a dozen years my junior). I would suggest it was our different neighborhoods that most defined what each of us experienced and observed.

I wrote a letter to Tim Russert in 2004, shortly after his book was published. I never met Mr. Russert, nor do I know if he ever read this letter. But this letter describes Buffalo's neighborhoods – and my experiences in them – in a way that both complements and contrasts with what Russert had described. I recommend *Big Russ and Me* – it is unfortunate that Russert died so young and there was never any opportunity to be in dialogue about our experiences.

Tim Russert
September 17, 2004
P. O. Box 5999
Washington D.C. 20016

Dear Mr. Russert:

I enjoyed reading your book, *"Big Russ & Me."* Your narrative concerning family and the South Park Community was quite insightful and thought provoking. Your description of your working class roots and your journey in becoming a preeminent news commentator (my description), moderator and political analyst is inspiring. It is always good to hear of a "Buffalo Boy" making good — really good. Your book has stimulated me to offer some comments and reflections on my years in Buffalo (1938-1962). Your book evoked memories of my own working-class youth in Buffalo. Though there are some similarities in our Buffalo experiences (I also worked for the Buffalo Sanitation Department) there are several differences between your experiences and those that I remember that I would like to offer as a means of contrast.

I am older than you—born in 1938 in Buffalo. Thus, I do remember most of the 1940's as well as the 1950's. There were still street cars in Buffalo in the forties. Few families owned autos —my father (an Italian immigrant) didn't own an automobile until 1957. At that time I was 19 years old and too occupied with attending and paying for college to afford a car of my own. I attended Buffalo State College. It was closer to my home than was my high school (Hutch-Tech). There was no tuition at that time and I lived at home, as there was no board to pay. Without public education there would have been little opportunity to attend college.

Buffalo - A Collection of Urban Villages

Jokes and weather aside, Buffalo was an interesting and a vital place in which to be raised. Buffalo was big enough to be urban and yet sufficiently decentralized into neighborhoods so that we could get to know people and in return become known and cared for by relatives, neighbors, long time friends and even local merchants. I believe Buffalo was a collection of urban villages. I lived on the "West Side," where the Italian community was located. There were relatively few non-Italians on Busti Avenue (parallel to Niagara Avenue and near the Peace Bridge). During the forties my world consisted of all Italians—a lot of community — but little diversity.

In 1946, my family moved to the Grant Street and Forest Avenue area which is also considered the West Side, but very different from "Busti" and the deep West Side. The deep West Side resembled a village from Italy—actually Sicily- transported to Buffalo. Everyone I knew not only was Italian, but was most likely to be Sicilian and obviously Catholic. When we moved to Grant Street the neighborhood was mixed with few Catholics and few Italians. I felt like an outsider among "Americans" whose ethnicity I could not identify, while it was easy to be pegged as an Italian (Dago, Wop) or worse, and a "Cat-Lick" as well. It seemed like it took forever (actually the better part of a year and many fist fights) to be accepted by the kids in the neighborhood.

My point is that there were several "West Sides'" and they differed in the character of their residents. The deep West Side Italian/Sicilian; Grant Street was mixed, Black Rock was mostly Polish and Delaware Park area was old line Anglo Hertel was a Jewish area. In your book, South Park was described as predominantly, if not, exclusively Irish. Was it so?

For me in the fifties, South Park was a million miles away, and as far as I was concerned it could have been near Rochester. Buffalo was, and remains, quite different than the Washington area where I have resided since 1975. You are correct; the Friday night fish fry was and remains an institution. My kids and now my grandkids always look forward to a fish fry when we visit family and friends in the Buffalo area. Invariably they exclaim "did you see the size of the fish." I also remember Birch Beer which I used to drink on tap in the saloon where my uncle used to stop after work. He had beer and treated me to birch beer. 1 don't ever remember drinking birch beer except in a saloon. You mentioned Simon Pure and Iroquois beers. My favorites were Genesee Cream Ale (Jenny) and O' Keefe which I used to get in Fort Erie or Crystal Beach when I was old enough— 18-year-olds could legally drink, but of course some of us started earlier.

Family

My father, Joe Marando was an Italian immigrant who attended school in Italy until the third grade when his father took him out of school to tend goats. He made sure that his six children, of which I am the eldest, all had the opportunity to attend college. All of us did. He worked hard so that we could go to school and get the education he was denied. He never overcame not being educated, but he took great pride in his kids' education.

My mother was the daughter of Italian immigrants. She was born in the Italian section of Buffalo called Dante Place. She attended school through the seventh grade, until she had to go to work. She was a great cook and fed not only her family and but many of the neighborhood kids as well. To this day, many of those "kids" of sixty years ago still remember being fed at our home. No one was ever turned away hungry. She was able to marry table and community in a way that I have not seen since.

Public Education

I attended public schools. For my family, Catholic schools required tuition that we were unable or unwilling to pay. The only formal Catholic education I received was Tuesday afternoon catechism class for one hour. My impression was that the working-class Italian Catholics related to the Church much differently than did the Irish kids. There was a strong anti-cleric feeling among the Italian males that I knew. The priests in the church I attended at that time were Irish and I felt they were from another world.

The priests in my experience had no significant role in my development or education. Actually, two public school teachers at P.S. 52 had dramatic impact on my development as a person and the choice I made to enter the field of education. One was a "Gym" teacher who came to understand me as well as anyone. He understood that I could not run very well because I contracted polio as an infant. He guided me into swimming in which I could perform reasonably well—certainly no Michael Phelps. He also had a hand in my appointment as captain of the swim team at PS 52. (See: attached photo and related testimonial.) The other teacher was Ms. Reiman who recognized my passion for social studies and was the launching pad for my going on to earn a Ph.D. in Political Science at Michigan State University. Only years after leaving P.S. 52 did I come to know that Mr. Speidel and Ms. Reiman were Jewish. Ironic that the teachers that had the most influence upon me were not Catholic, nor Italian. I will always be grateful to what they imparted to me and the memory of them.

It was when I went to Buffalo Technical High School in 1952 (Clinton St. east of Michigan Avenue) later named Hutchinson-Central Technical High School (Elmwood and Chippewa) did I really meet a cross section of kids from all over the city. To gain admission we had to test into "Tech" and if we didn't keep up our grades or did not behave properly, we would be sent back to our district high school. Academic competition at Tech was quite serious and the school gave me a sense of confidence that I could compete academically. The boys were bright. At that time Tech was an all boy's school, but has since become coeducational.

Tech provided an integrated environment and a student body diversity that I could never have been exposed to at the district school (Lafayette) on the West Side. In fact, it was in High School that I got my first and only opportunity to visit South Park High for a swimming meet. Although I knew there was a South Park section of the city I had no reason or means of transportation to get there. I still remember that South Park High in 1956 had the most phenomenal swimmer in the city. His name was Dick Hutchinson and he rewrote the record books. As great a swimmer as he was, I don't believe he went to college, but went to work for Bethlehem Steel. A great talent lost. Although I have not seen him since high school, he remains a topic of conversation when a my former "Tech" swim teammate and I get together for a beer or two.

After Buffalo State, I attended graduate school at Michigan State University. I studied state and local government. I wrote my Masters thesis on the effects of <u>Baker v. Carr</u> on the Erie County delegation to the New York State Assembly. Among those I interviewed were all Erie County state legislators. I came to value and enjoy in-depth elite interviews as a method of political inquiry. I have learned a lot from politicians and public administrators. I received a Ph.D. in 1967 and started an academic career in 1967 that began at the University of Arizona, on to the University of Georgia and finishing at the University of Maryland, College Park. Again, I was exposed to exceptional teachers who not only knew their stuff but took a personal interest in me. Although I never met Daniel Moynihan I am familiar with much of his work.

Work

My father also worked for the Buffalo Sanitation Department and he retired from there in 1975, He was a "roller" taking the garbage cans out from the back yards to the curb during the middle of the night. His work on the rolling job was completed before he went to his "second" job as a janitor and fireman to stoke the coal furnace at a public elementary school. I helped him when the weather was particularly bad and rolling through the snow would make finishing his route especially long so that he would get to his second job on time. I can remember quite clearly seeing rats jump off the cans into the snow, forming tunnels in all directions.

On occasion, I worked as a temp for the Buffalo Sanitation Department. I worked on a garbage truck or should I say behind the truck. What I liked most about that job was that we could go home after we finished—which consisted of only 3 or 4 hours of work for a full day's pay. I also worked every summer for the City Parks Department as a lifeguard. That was a great job—good pay, prestige and a lot of girls who thought we were cute. The supervisor of the city pools was Mr. Joseph "Joe" Sweeney who was from South Park, He was also the swim coach at "Tech" and built a swimming powerhouse in part because he got his 'boys" lifeguard jobs so that we could practice during the summer as well as during the school year.

I found no work particularly hard as long as it supplemented my education and that I knew it was not permanent. I felt sorry for those guys that had to go to the factories or work construction day in and day out.

You are correct, Buffalo and the community it was, had much to offer kids. I am particularly thankful to the many public school teachers who gave much of themselves to help kids, many of whom spoke broken English.

I have been retired from the University of Maryland, College Park since 2001. To think that I have a title of Professor Emeritus is both personally satisfying and ironic given my Buffalo experiences and what I might have become. The fact that I didn't end up at the Ford plant, in construction, or in organized crime, is testimony to many caring people who offered much needed encouragement and guidance.

You are obviously proud of your father as I am sure he is of you. It is obvious that in large part, by standing upon the shoulders (sweat, hard work and love) of fathers such as "Big Russ" and "Mr. Joe," that we can have fulfilling lives and obtain goals that might have been beyond our expectations.

Thanks for sharing your story,

Vincent L. Marando

Columbia, MD 21044

APPENDIX C:

OPENING THE DOORS TO THE "ACADEMIC" BIG LEAGUES

In the February 9, 2014 edition of the *Washington Post* there was an obituary for Professor Emeritus Robert A. Dahl of Yale University. Robert Dahl was a preeminent political scientist during the 1950's and 1960s, while I was an undergraduate and graduate student. The obituary made reference to his having written several classic books, and made specific mention of his seminal work, published in 1961, entitled *"Who Governs?"*.

After 50 years what struck me about this when I read his obituary was that I had read this book very shortly after it had been published. The circumstances which allowed me to read these books and many others, was stimulated by Professors Charles R. Adrian and Charles O. Press – "Chuck" and "Charlie". I took classes from Professors Adrian and Press during my first year as a graduate student at Michigan State University. They were the faculty members who became my graduate school mentors.

But to get to Chuck and Charlie, it's helpful to go back a bit farther. I earned my B.S. in Education from Buffalo State College in the spring of 1960; I began full-time classroom teaching that fall. While I began teaching, I also took a graduate class at Buffalo State; the course was State and Local Government taught by instructor Raymond Stone. Stone was a Princeton-trained scholar of political science. He was an outstanding teacher. While working for the City of Buffalo I had been exposed to politics, yet I did not understand or grasp the nature of the politics in which I was enmeshed. His course raised the level of scholarship and study that I was accustomed to as an undergraduate student at Buffalo State. He brought home the linkage and difference between practicing politics and studying Political Science.

While a student in high school and college, in the late 1950s, I was a lifeguard and later a supervisor of a City of Buffalo aquatic facility. I had gained local government experience through my employment with the City of Buffalo, particularly the experience of managing this recreational facility. At the time, I did not grasp that I was enmeshed in a political system because I was managing a city facility. I looked upon managing the swim facility and playground as "a summer job" — a means of income to finance my education.

But there was an important measure of politics woven into working for Buffalo Parks and Recreation; I did not know it at the time, but the experience I gained there would later serve me well as a political science graduate student.

For example, the minimum age for becoming a city lifeguard was 17 years old, but I was not yet 17 when I was hired as a lifeguard. The decisions to hire lifeguards were based on passing tests and professional criteria; politics and political connections were not sufficient to be hired for that position. City pool assignments were ostensibly made by administrative criteria – but did political influence also have a role?

What I did not grasp at the time was the link between two City of Buffalo positions that Joseph Sweeney occupied. During the summer, Mr. Sweeney was City Parks and Recreation Director. During the school year, he was my swim coach at Hutch-Tech High School. Joe Sweeney built a swimming team powerhouse in part by "facilitating" the process that allowed Hutch-Tech swim team members to obtain summer lifeguard and management positions at the City's aquatic facilities.

Was my early hire "administrative oversight" or "politics"?

During Professor Stone's class, we read a Charles Adrian's *Governing Urban America*, which shed light on many aspects of local government that applied to my summer work experience with the City of Buffalo. When I read his textbook, I was absolutely astonished that state and local government was a defined area of academic political science study. Little did I know that Charles Adrian's work had redefined inquiry into state and local government in the United States.

I thought "Wow... I can study politics and have a career teaching high school social studies." I would be qualified to teach state and local politics as part of a high school American government curriculum.

My goal was to obtain a master's degree in Political Science.

I decided to enroll at Michigan State University (MSU) in the fall of 1961 as a graduate student; Adrian's textbook on state and local government was the trigger that spurred me to make application to MSU, where he was a professor. I came to understand that Charles R. Adrian was not only a Professor of Political Science; he was the preeminent scholar of state and local government in the U.S.

Professor Adrian was one of the most imposing and commanding persons I've ever met. He could have fulfilled Hollywood's central casting requirements for a five-star general in a war movie. Indeed, among the graduate students Adrian was referred to as "five-star." General George Patton could have taken lessons on how to look like a leader from Charles R. Adrian. He was ramrod straight, tall, broad shouldered, with angular facial features and blonde hair worn in a crew cut. His speech was measured, and always precise.

In my first year at MSU I took six classes, among which was Professor Adrian's urban government theory class. In Professor Adrian's seminar being prepared meant having read the "suggested" readings as well as the required weekly assignments. As a student, I was being exposed to a professor who was defining the field of local government as he was conducting a seminar. Weekly, we would be reading his published journal articles along with the classic works of preeminent scholars-- three of whom went on to became Nobel Laureates. Adrian's research was cutting-edge and extremely well-written. His writings on local government read as if they were novels. His literature and book reviews were themselves contributions to the field, often providing more insight than the material under review.

Later in my studies at Michigan State University, Chuck Adrian offered me an opportunity to take an independent reading class in state and local government. I was not a particularly outstanding student, but I did gain his attention in a previous seminar by raising questions that struck at the heart of a theory he was advocating. As I recall, in class we were applying Thomas Schelling's Cold War strategic game theory to the politics of local government.[79] The applied game theory offered much insight into understanding local government politics, yet it seemed to me that it had a glaring gap. In my naïveté, I asked how does one know when the game of politics is over? Doesn't the game start all over, once the first game is "finished"? Political strategies and games are never over. The games evolve into new games, over and over again. These comments struck Adrian as insightful. He questioned me at length and the discussion went back and forth for quite a time. I had said something insightful but did not grasp my own insight. I certainly didn't tell Adrian I didn't know the full scope of the theory. After the game theory exchange, Professor Adrian took a special interest in me as a student. I was a raw first-year graduate student who saw things from the "street-level"; or as we would have said on campus, from "field observation."

I also became Chuck Adrian's teaching assistant. I recall an incident in a large American government lecture class of 300 students. Professor Adrian noticed as he was lecturing one day that a student was reading a newspaper. He stopped lecturing and waited for the student to look up

---

79 Schelling (1921-2016) won the Nobel Prize in Economic Sciences in 2005 for this work; he was also the basis for the main character in Stanley Kubrick's 1964 movie *Dr. Strangelove Or: How I Learned to Stop Worrying and Love the Bomb*. In an odd twist, Prof. Schelling would become my colleague in the College of Behavioral and Social Sciences at the University of Maryland in 1990, when he took a joint appointment in the Department of Economics and the School of Public Policy.

from the newspaper. Several moments passed while all 299 other students viewed the student reading the newspaper. When the student reading the paper grasped that the lecture had stopped and looked up, Adrian said "you've insulted me and the entire class. Leave, and you may return when you are ready to pay attention." For the remainder of the semester, the students attending Adrian's lectures were attentive to a fault.[80]

Most importantly, in the 1964 spring quarter I was offered an independent studies class with Chuck Adrian. I was his only student – we were one-on-one. We met weekly to discuss recent and classic books in the field of state and local politics. The blending of academic and actual work experience in local government was fascinating and enlightening to me and I suspect to Professor Adrian as well. There was no rationale for him to give me undivided attention once a week in a one-hour session, except that I was speaking to theory on the basis of practice and experience.

I didn't realize it at that time, but I was blending theory and practice. I didn't quite grasp why "blending" was an attraction for Professor Adrian; I felt I was just a raw graduate student, relying upon several years of local government experience as a basis for pursuing an academic career. It must have hit him that I was a bit different than most other students, who possessed exclusively academic knowledge of local government. He selected me and gave me the opportunity for an independent studies class that had profound impact on my education and career.

But though I came to MSU primarily to study with Charles "Chuck" Adrian, I got a "twofer" – a Chuck and a Charlie. Adrian collaborated with Charlie Press in many phases of scholarship; they had co-authored publications and joint research projects and had done much government consulting together. First Adrian and then Press served as Chairs of the Political

---

80 As Adrian and I became better acquainted, he confided in me that his state and local government textbook, published by McGraw-Hill, was the book that provided income to purchase his home. He jokingly referred to his home as "the house McGraw-Hill built." I realized that he was quite modest and basically a shy person, which was often interpreted by other students as being distant and aloof.

Science Department during my graduate student tenure. In addition, they were close friends. I ended up studying with both while in residence MSU.

I took a seminar in state and local government from Charlie Press during the 1963 fall quarter, when he took over a class that Chuck Adrian had been scheduled to teach. I enjoyed the class. Charlie Press was more informal and lot more policy-oriented than was Adrian; and though I was far from the very best student in the class, he was an engaging and stimulating professor who encouraged me in my studies.

At the end of my first year at MSU, Charlie Press agreed to serve as the chairman of my master's thesis committee. When Charles Adrian accepted a faculty position at the University of California at Riverside in 1966, Charlie Press total. Without missing a beat, Charlie Press had become my major professor; he continued as my mentor for the remainder of my studies at MSU.

The United States Supreme Court had passed the landmark state legislative reapportionment case of _Baker v. Carr_ in the spring of 1962. I wanted to use this case to study the impact of reapportionment on the Erie County delegation to the New York State Assembly. Charlie's knowledge of state government reform was absolutely essential for completing my thesis while I was living in New York.[81] Charlie Press not only provided direction as I wrote my MA thesis from a distance, he also went way beyond what was required of the chair in guiding me. Working with Charlie on my master's thesis transformed me from a fledgling graduate student into a budding scholar.

Charlie Press' activity in guiding me through the thesis process provided the basis for a relationship that evolved into an academic partnership. Upon completing the master's degree, Charlie guided me in applying and interviewing for other opportunities, which led to my being awarded a Ford Fellowship with the Michigan State Legislature. The Fellowship provided me with a great opportunity to see the political process at work.

81 By that time, I had married Patty and was also holding a full-time teaching position in Niagara Falls.

The Ford Fellowship's compensation was $400 a month in 1964. This sum provided a living wage at the time that allowed me to make a living as a graduate student, especially since I was now married and my wife Patti and I were expecting our first daughter, Marianne.

I had completed my M.A. and continued on into the Ph.D. program; Charlie Press was my mentor guiding me through this new phase. He was always there, both when I needed him and when I wasn't sure that I needed him – but he knew I needed him. He would come to his office at the Kellogg Center, which he allowed me to use when he was not there. At the time he had two offices, and one was virtually mine. I was the only graduate student who had sole use of a private office fit for a Full Professor. Each time he saw me he asked, "what have you written since the last time we met?"

Charles Adrian left Michigan State University to take a position at the University of California at Riverside while I was pursuing my doctorate. His leaving MSU was a loss for the University, and for me especially. Before Adrian departed, he was on my dissertation proposal committee to research the political integration of the Detroit metropolitan area. I have kept his written comments on my dissertation proposal among my writings and publications for all these years. He commented that my use of the term "my interviewees" was quite possessive – but he interpreted my loose language as a sign of commitment to the research. Adrian was not only a gifted writer; he also read between the lines.[82]

Adrian's departure from the University was not as big a disaster as I had anticipated; Charlie Press more than adequately guided me through the remainder of my graduate career. Without Charlie Press' guidance, I am not sure what the outcome of my graduate program would have been.

When I was awarded a position at the University of Arizona, I did not have to interview in-person: being the student of Professors Press and Adrian was enough of a recommendation for an to be appointed as an

---

82 On several occasions I observed Chuck in East Lansing bookstores browsing through books on writing. Even though he was a Distinguished Full Professor he continued to work on his writing skills – which were quite formidable – throughout his career.

Assistant Professor at the University of Arizona in 1967; without being interviewed in person.

I came to realize after accepting a position as an assistant professor at the University of Arizona that there was more emphasis on research and publishing involved in being a professor at a major state university. The emphasis on research as well as teaching continued after leaving Arizona to accept more senior positions at the University of Georgia and the University of Maryland, College Park. Good teaching was expected at these universities, but in fact, it was research publications that garnered pay raises and promotions. Publishing was an absolute necessity at all three universities. I had to publish, or as the cliché states, perish. But that is another story for another time.

From Ms. Reiman to Raymond Stone to Chuck Adrian to Charlie Press – step by step, it was the gifted teachers who took the time to make a connection with me that got me from Grant Street to the hallowed halls of academia, and a career as a professor. I look back on each of them with gratitude – I have no idea what my life would have become without their encouragement and willingness to guide me my to the next level.

APPENDIX D:

THE GAMES WE PLAYED

We played on the sidewalk, backyards and street when I lived o Busti Avenue. There were no nearby playgrounds.

Relievio

My favorite game was Ring-a-Relievio, which was a shorthand way of saying, "I relieve you." You may have been captured but I will relieve – or free – you. In my mind this was a war game based on us (the good guys) taking prisoners away from them (the enemy).

"Relievio" was an amalgamation of hide-and-go-seek and tag. Players would be divided up into two teams. There was a captain for each team who then picked team members. Players for each team were selected alternately; the teams would be relatively equal in the quality of the combined capabilities of players who might range in age from seven to fifteen years old.

After the choice of which team was to start by hiding and which team was to search was made, members of the search team turned to face a telephone pole, covered their eyes and counted to 100 before they would seek the team that had gone into hiding. Members of the team that was to hide ran in all directions throughout the block and hid in backyards, among bushes or anywhere else considered not to be an easy place to be found by a member of the other team.

When a hiding team member was tagged, he was returned to a square drawn on the sidewalk in which he was placed in "prison" and guarded by a seeking team member. However, there was an opportunity to free prisoners from "prison" when an uncaptured member of the hiding team would run back to the prison square and step within the drawn marked square on the sidewalk before being tagged by one of the seekers. When the hiding team member freed those who were in prison, he would yell "I relieve you" thereby giving the game the name "Relievio." When members were released from prison they could run throughout the neighborhood and hide again. The game would end would end when all hiding team members were captured and placed in "prison."

Nip

"Nip" was a game that may have been invented locally in Buffalo. Why the name "nip" was chosen is not certain to anyone who played the game; With no evidence I believed "nip" may have been used as a derogatory term for Japanese, since as players hit the "nip" they pretended to hit the enemy.

Nip was a game played by boys at least eight years old and more often older.

The game consisted of taking a wooden broom handle and cutting two pieces from it. The first piece would be a stick that would be used as a bat; it was anywhere from 18 inches to two feet long (not dissimilar to the stick used in stickball in New York City). The second portion of the broom handle was the piece called a "nip" that was cut to about four inches long, with the ends tapered with a knife to have points. The object was to use the stick portion of the broom handle as a bat to strike the end of the tapered shorter piece of broom handle. By hitting the end of the nip and striking it, as it rose and flipped in the air.

Home plate was generally a telephone pole or lamppost from where the first strike was taken. A player was permitted to hit the nip three times. Each player in turn was given three hits at the nip. After hitting the nip where it landed after the first strike the player would advance to the nip and have a second opportunity hit the nip further. This was followed by a third hit the nip. Of course, some players didn't hit the nip all three times; a boy may have struck out once, twice, or even three times by missing the nip as it flipped into the air. The accomplished players would have hit the nip three times.

The furthest distance from home plate that the nip advanced after three hits determined the winner. The distance from the home base pole to the spot where the nip landed after the third strike was measured by the length of the batting stick. A batter – under the watchful eyes of all players – would measure the distance by flipping the batting stick end over end all the way back to home. The second player would get a similar opportunity to do the same.

Sometimes the distance was not very far because younger players only hit the nip once or may have missed the nip altogether. In such cases there was no question who hit the nip furthest from home base and would be considered the winner. When the game involved the older more athletic older players in their teens the nip was hit three times by all batters, and the nip landed many stick lengths (yards) from home plate. The measuring of the distance back to home plate was always awash with great enthusiasm and sometimes arguments about the measured distances. The winner was crowned as neighborhood "nip" king.